STING AND THE POLICE

Tempo: A Rowman & Littlefield Music Series on Rock, Pop, and Culture
Series Editor: Scott Calhoun

Tempo: A Rowman & Littlefield Music Series on Rock, Pop, and Culture offers titles that explore rock and popular music through the lens of social and cultural history, revealing the dynamic relationship between musicians, music, and their milieu. Like other major art forms, rock and pop music comment on their cultural, political, and even economic situation, reflecting the technological advances, psychological concerns, religious feelings, and artistic trends of their times. Contributions to the Tempo series are the ideal introduction to major pop and rock artists and genres.

Titles in the Series

Bob Dylan: American Troubadour, by Donald Brown
Bon Jovi: America's Ultimate Band, by Margaret Olson
British Invasion: The Crosscurrents of Musical Influence, by Simon Philo
Bruce Springsteen: American Poet and Prophet, by Donald L. Deardorff II
The Clash: The Only Band That Mattered, by Sean Egan
Kris Kristofferson: Country Highwayman, by Mary G. Hurd
Patti Smith: America's Punk Rock Rhapsodist, by Eric Wendell
Paul Simon: An American Tune, by Cornel Bonca
Ska: The Rhythm of Liberation, by Heather Augustyn
Sting and The Police, by Aaron J. West

STING AND THE POLICE

Walking in Their Footsteps

Aaron J. West

ROWMAN & LITTLEFIELD
Lanham • Boulder • New York • London

Published by Rowman & Littlefield
A wholly owned subsidiary of The Rowman & Littlefield Publishing Group,
Inc.
4501 Forbes Boulevard, Suite 200, Lanham, Maryland 20706
www.rowman.com

Unit A, Whitacre Mews, 26-34 Stannary Street, London SE11 4AB

British Library Cataloguing in Publication Information Available

Library of Congress Cataloging-in-Publication Data

West, Aaron J.
Sting and The Police : walking in their footsteps / Aaron J. West.
pages cm. — (Tempo : a Rowman & Littlefield music series on rock, pop, and culture)
Includes bibliographical references and index.
ISBN 978-0-8108-8490-8 (hardback : alk. paper) — ISBN 978-0-8108-8491-5 (ebook) 1. Police
(Musical group) 2. Sting (Musician) 3. Rock music—1981-1990—History and criticism. I. Title.
ML421.P67W47 2015
782.42166092'2—dc23
2015015451

♾ ™ The paper used in this publication meets the minimum requirements of
American National Standard for Information Sciences Permanence of Paper
for Printed Library Materials, ANSI/NISO Z39.48-1992.

Printed in the United States of America

CONTENTS

FOREWORD

Scott Calhoun, Series Editor

The following exploration of Sting and The Police as artists—as jazz-, funk-, reggae-, and folk-pop artists, specifically—gets it right about how a three-piece combo can turn alchemic. Stewart Copeland, Andy Summers, and Gordon Matthew Sumner, or Sting, brought their musical curiosities and complex personalities together to form a new wave of astute, infectious English song craft, while giving audiences years of thrilling performances. Aaron J. West gets it right too, about the chemistry of a complicated musical artist who trends toward the restless, virtuosic type, as is true of Sting. Seeming to enjoy the chase of craft as much as the adulation of the crowd, The Police's potency came from skillful compounding of musical styles already marked by strong grooves, inventive tempos, and playfulness. The music The Police made, and that Sting continues to make, has satisfied the literate and literary, as well the mainstream appetite for something eminently fun to sing and dance to. But Sting's thirst for a greater, more singular pursuit of craft and crowd sent him on many more cultural quests after The Police, looking for the pop hooks, world beats, activist heroics, and even stage roles offered by film and theater, to satiate the artist.

Sometimes accused of appropriation by critics who lean toward purists, The Police's music has nevertheless endured. It has inspired many post-1980s artists who had the good fortune of composing their songs in times when borrowing, referencing, and sampling was de rigueur. At times accused of affectation, Sting, never the shy nor demure performer, has turned any such complaints to his advantage, commanding our attention when on a new project by promising to tip the balance from showmanship toward sophistication. This study presents Sting and The Police by choosing a different path of presentation. Pop legends they are, with storied lives and plenty of laurels to show for it. But West's perspective is drawn to seeing their rise to acclaim and influence in popular music history as the acts of artists choosing their colors, their brush strokes, and their canvases, intentionally assembling the pieces to make something brilliantly new.

TIMELINE

World and Cultural Events	*Sting, Andy Summers, and Stewart Copeland's Lives and Careers*
December 1942: In the midst of World War II, over sixty U-boats are sunk.	**December 1942**: Andrew James Summers is born December 31 at the edge of the river Wyre in Lancashire (Poulton-le-Fylde), near Blackpool, England.
January 1945: The Soviet Red Army liberates the Birkenau and Auschwitz concentration camps.	
August 1945: The United States bombs Hiroshima and Nagasaki with atomic weapons. World War II ends soon after.	
July 1946: U.S. nuclear testing begins at Bikini Atoll in Micronesia. Sting protests these kinds of experiments with "La Belle Dame Sans Regrets" in 1996.	
February 1947: Voice of America begins transmitting into	

World and Cultural Events	*Sting, Andy Summers, and Stewart Copeland's Lives and Careers*
the Soviet Union and its satellites. These broadcasts will influence generations of Eastern European and Russian musicians.	
March 1948: Arturo Toscanini, during his television debut, conducts the NBC Symphony, performing the works of Richard Wagner.	
April 1950: The Group Areas Acts passes in South Africa, formally segregating the races. By the 1980s, performers will play a number of anti-apartheid shows.	
October 1951: *I Love Lucy* debuts on CBS, and Winston Churchill is re-elected prime minister of the United Kingdom.	**October 1951**: Gordon Matthew Thomas Sumner (Sting) is born in Wallsend, Tyneside, Tyne and Wear, England. His childhood in Wallsend will be the inspiration for multiple songs and even a Broadway show.
July 1952: Mickey Mantle hits his first grand slam.	**July 1952**: Stewart Armstrong Copeland is born in Alexandria, Virginia, on July 16.
April 1953: Frank Sinatra and Nelson Riddle begin their iconic recordings for Capitol Records.	**1953**: The young Andy Summers is listening to AFN radio, which plays American jazz.
May 1954: *Brown v. Board of Education of Topeka* bans racial segregation in U.S. public schools.	
September 1955: *Gunsmoke*, television's longest-running	**1955**: Andy Summers is given his first guitar by his uncle Jim. A

World and Cultural Events	Sting, Andy Summers, and Stewart Copeland's Lives and Careers
western, debuts on CBS. Sting will cite this as one of his favorite programs as a child.	lodger named David Ellis helps him tune it.
February 1956: Elvis Presley has his first hit with "Heartbreak Hotel."	**November 1956**: As Queen Elizabeth II rides by, Sting greets her by waving a Union Jack. She waves back.
January 1957: The Cavern Club opens in Liverpool; it will become an early performance venue for The Beatles.	
August 1957: *American Bandstand* premiers.	
October 1957: The Soviet Union launches Sputnik 1 into orbit.	**October 1957**: Summers buys a Gibson ES-175 in London.
	1958: Summers buys a Gibson ES-335. Eventually, there will be an Andy Summers signature model of this guitar.
	July 1958: The U.S. Marines land in Beirut, Lebanon, to protect the existing pro-Western government. The Copeland family will leave for London soon after.
April 1960: *Ben-Hur* wins a number of Academy Awards, including Best Picture. Stewart Copeland will premiere a live-performance score for an earlier film version of *Ben-Hur* in 2014.	
August 1961: Construction of the Berlin Wall begins.	

World and Cultural Events	*Sting, Andy Summers, and Stewart Copeland's Lives and Careers*
August 1962: President Kennedy orders a blockade of Cuba in order to prevent the establishment of Soviet missile bases.	
	1964: Andy Summers joins Zoot Money's Big Roll Band.
	December 1965: Sting attends The Beatles' arrival at Newcastle City Hall.
	March 1967: Sting attends a concert by The Jimi Hendrix Experience at Club A' Go Go in Newcastle.
	July 1967: Summers, along with musicians from Zoot Money's Big Roll Band, creates Dantalian's Chariot, a contemporary psychedelic band.
August 1967: Brian Epstein, manager for The Beatles, dies.	**August 1967**: Copeland attends a concert by The Jimi Hendrix Experience at the Saville Theatre in London.
	May 1968: Summers joins the early progressive rock group, Soft Machine.
	July 1968: Summers is dismissed from Soft Machine.
	August 1968: Summers travels to California and joins Eric Burdon and The Animals.

World and Cultural Events

Sting, Andy Summers, and Stewart Copeland's Lives and Careers

October 1968: Summers jams with Jimi Hendrix at TTG Studios in Hollywood, California.

January 1969: The first Led Zeppelin album is released; The Beatles give their last public performance.

July 1969: Neil Armstrong becomes first man to walk on the moon.

August 1969: Woodstock Music Festival takes place.

December 1969: Tragic Rolling Stones' show at Altamont Raceway takes place.

April 1970: The first Earth Day is celebrated in the United States. In the following decade, Sting will become an advocate for environmentalism.

September 1970: Jimi Hendrix dies in London of drug-related complications.

March 1971: Paul Simon's "Bridge over Troubled Water" wins a Grammy Award for Song of the Year. Sting will tour with Simon forty-three years later.

March 1972: Northern Ireland is occupied by Britain. The resulting unrest will inspire "Invisible Sun."

1972: Along with keyboardist Gerry Richardson, Sting joins Earthrise.

World and Cultural Events	*Sting, Andy Summers, and Stewart Copeland's Lives and Careers*
November 1972: Atari introduces the arcade version of *Pong*, the first video game. Stewart Copeland will write the music for the video game *Spyro the Dragon* in 1998.	
January 1973: A ceasefire is signed in Vietnam. Ian Copeland, Stewart Copeland's brother, had fought in the war.	**1973**: Sting joins the Phoenix Jazzmen, a traditional jazz group from which he earns his nickname.
February 1973: *The Harder They Come*, starring Jimmy Cliff, increases the visibility of reggae in the United States.	
	May 1973: Stewart Copeland is the tour manager for Joan Armatrading's UK tour.
	November 1973: Andy Summers returns to London.
May 1974: India becomes the world's sixth nuclear power. The Police will perform in India during their 1980 world tour.	**1974**: Summers begins touring with actor and singer David Essex, Neil Sedaka, and Kevin Coyne.
August 1974: President Richard Nixon resigns.	
	October 1974: Last Exit begins rehearsing.
	December 1974: Copeland becomes the tour manager, and later drummer, for the progressive rock band, Curved Air.

World and Cultural Events

Sting, Andy Summers, and Stewart Copeland's Lives and Careers

October 1975: *Saturday Night Live* premieres with George Carlin as host. Sting will perform on *SNL* multiple times.

November 1976: Jimmy Carter is elected president of the United States.

1976: Curved Air records *Airbourne* with Stewart Copeland. Summers begins performing with Kevin Ayers.

December 1976: Copeland meets Sting after a Curved Air concert and gives him his phone number.

January 1977: Sting moves to London with his wife and child. By mid-January, Sting, Copeland, and Henry Padovani are rehearsing.

April 1977: The legendary disco club, Studio 54, opens in New York City.

May 1977: Andy Summers performs with Copeland and Sting in Strontium 90. Also, The Police, with Henry Padovani, release the single "Fall Out/Nothing Achieving."

July 1977: Andy Summers performs with The Police for the first time.

August 1977: Elvis Presley dies at Graceland.

World and Cultural Events	*Sting, Andy Summers, and Stewart Copeland's Lives and Careers*
September 1977: South African activist Steve Biko dies in police custody.	
October 1977: *Never Mind the Bollocks, Here's the Sex Pistols* is released on A&M Records. This company will also release all of The Police albums.	
	February 1978: The Police bleach their hair for a Wrigley's Spearmint chewing gum commercial. Their blonde hair will be a definitive part of their image.
	October 1978: The Police begin their first U.S. tour.
	November 1978: *Outlandos d'Amour* is released on A&M Records.
March 1979: The nuclear power plant at Three Mile Island, Pennsylvania, has an accidental release of radiation.	**March 1979**: The Police begin their second U.S. tour.
May 1979: Conservative politician Margaret Thatcher becomes new prime minister. Her conservative policies will draw the ire of many British performers, including Sting.	
	October 1979: *Reggatta de Blanc* is released.
December 1979: The Soviet Union invades Afghanistan.	

World and Cultural Events	*Sting, Andy Summers, and Stewart Copeland's Lives and Careers*
April 1980: A helicopter and a cargo plane collide in a disastrous attempt to rescue American hostages in Tehran.	**1980**: The Police are filmed during a world tour, which will result in *The Police: Around the World*.
	October 1980: *Zenyatta Mondatta* is released.
November 1980: Ronald Reagan is elected president of the United States.	
December 1980: John Lennon is shot in New York City.	
August 1981: MTV premieres with the Buggles' "Video Killed the Radio Star."	
	September 1981: Sting performs at the Theatre Royal for Amnesty International. Sting sings "Roxanne," "Message in a Bottle," and leads a performance of "I Shall Be Released" as a closing number. This is Sting's introduction to Amnesty International.
	October 1981: *Ghost in the Machine* is released. It hits No. 2 in the United States.
	1982: Stewart Copeland begins recording the soundtrack to *Rumble Fish*. His work will be nominated for a Golden Globe Award.

World and Cultural Events	*Sting, Andy Summers, and Stewart Copeland's Lives and Careers*
	October 1982: Andy Summers/ Robert Fripp's *I Advance Masked* is released.
November 1982: Michael Jackson's *Thriller* debuts.	
March 1983: The first compact discs are sold in North America and Europe.	**1983**: Summers publishes a photography book titled *Throb*.
June 1983: Famine in Ethiopia begins reaching epic proportions.	**June 1983**: *Synchronicity* is released. It will be The Police's best-selling album and one of the most iconic albums of the 1980s.
	August 1983: The Police perform at Shea Stadium, and Sting proclaims, "This is it."
October 1983: The United States invades Grenada.	
	March 1984: The Police complete their final world tour in Melbourne, Australia (until their reunion).
May 1984: The Soviet Union withdraws from the Olympic Games.	
	September 1984: Andy Summers/Robert Fripp's *Bewitched* is released.
November 1984: Bob Geldof's Band Aid releases "Do They Know It's Christmas?" in an attempt to aid starving Ethiopians. Sting participates in the recording.	

World and Cultural Events	Sting, Andy Summers, and Stewart Copeland's Lives and Careers
March 1985: USA for Africa debuts "We Are the World."	
	May 1985: Filming begins for *Bring on the Night*, a documentary promoting Sting's new solo career.
	June 1985: Sting's first solo album, *The Dream of the Blue Turtles*, is released.
	July 1985: Sting performs at Live Aid. He performs with only Branford Marsalis on saxophone.
October 1985: Terrorists hijack the *Achille Lauro*, an Italian cruise liner.	
	November 1985: *Every Breath You Take: The Singles*, a compilation album, is released. It features "Don't Stand so Close to Me '86," a maligned remake of the original.
January 1986: The space shuttle *Challenger* explodes.	
April 1986: The Chernobyl nuclear accident occurs in the Soviet Union.	
	June 1986: The Police perform three shows for the Conspiracy of Hope Tour. These will be their last performances until 2003.
	July 1986: Sting's excellent live album, *Bring on the Night,*

World and Cultural Events	*Sting, Andy Summers, and Stewart Copeland's Lives and Careers*
	debuts. It features inventive arrangements and superlative performances of his greatest hits.
November 1986: An American secret initiative is discovered, revealing the diversion of funds from arms sales to Nicaraguan Contras. Sting will later write "Fragile," inspired by the death of an American civil engineer killed by the Contras in 1987.	
January 1987: Aretha Franklin is the first woman to be inducted into the Rock and Roll Hall of Fame. The Police will be inducted in 2003.	**1987**: Andy Summers's *XYZ* is released. Summers's attempt at mainstream success does not attain critical or commercial acceptance.
June 1987: An Iranian airliner is shot down by a U.S. Navy ship in the Persian Gulf.	
	October 1987: Sting's . . . *Nothing Like the Sun* debuts.
	November 1987: Sting meets Jean-Pierre Dutilleux and flies to the Xingu reservation to meet Chief Raoni.
	December 1987: The film *Wall Street* is released, featuring a soundtrack written by Stewart Copeland.
January 1988: Broadway's longest-running show, *The Phantom of the Opera*, opens.	**1988**: Andy Summers debuts *Mysterious Barricades*.

World and Cultural Events	Sting, Andy Summers, and Stewart Copeland's Lives and Careers

Sting will attempt his own Broadway show in 2014.

August 1988: Al-Qaeda is formed by Osama bin Laden.

November 1988: Stewart Copeland's ballet, *Emilio*, debuts.

December 1988: Pan Am 747 is destroyed from a terrorist bomb, crashing in Lockerbie, Scotland. Nearly three hundred people are killed.

March 1989: The *Exxon Valdez* spills 11 million gallons of oil into Alaska's Prince William Sound.

1989: Andy Summers releases *The Golden Wire*.

April 1989: Sting and Chief Raoni meet Pope John Paul II at the Vatican. Raoni and Sting had conducted a series of press conferences to draw attention to issues in the Amazonian rain forest.

October 1989: Stewart Copeland's new band, Animal Logic, releases *Animal Logic*. His *Holy Blood and Crescent Moon* debuts in Cleveland as well.

November 1989: The Berlin Wall falls.

December 1989: *The Simpsons* premieres. Sting will help sing "We're Sending Our Love Down the Well" in 1992. The part was

World and Cultural Events	Sting, Andy Summers, and Stewart Copeland's Lives and Careers

originally offered to Bruce Springsteen.

February 1990: Nelson Mandela is freed after twenty-seven years in prison.

1990: Summers's *Charming Snakes* debuts. The album is steeped in contemporary jazz fusion.

August 1990: Kuwait is invaded by Iraqi forces, which will draw the United States into the conflict.

November 1990: Margaret Thatcher resigns as British Prime Minister.

January 1991: Sting's *Soul Cages* is released to mixed reviews. The album is more introspective than most listeners expect from a Sting album.

July 1991: Animal Logic releases their final album, *Animal Logic II*.

August 1991: Summers's *World Gone Strange* debuts.

September 1991: Nirvana's single, "Smells Like Teen Spirit," is released. The drummer is Dave Grohl, who, with the Foo Fighters, will host Stewart Copeland during a tour in 2008.

April 1992: A tribute to Freddie Mercury is held at Wembley Stadium, raising millions for AIDS research.

World and Cultural Events

Sting, Andy Summers, and Stewart Copeland's Lives and Careers

November 1992: Bill Clinton is elected 42nd president of the United States.

1993: *Invisible Threads* with John Etheridge and Andy Summers is released.

March 1993: *Ten Summoner's Tales* debuts to rave reviews.

September 1993: *Message in a Box* is released. This box set contains the majority of The Police's studio recordings.

February 1994: Steve Fossett becomes the first person to make a solo flight across the Pacific Ocean in a balloon.

April 1994: Kurt Cobain commits suicide by a self-inflicted gunshot.

August 1994: A cease-fire is declared by the IRA in Northern Ireland.

October 1994: Pope John Paul II visits the United States.

April 1995: The Alfred P. Murrah Federal Building in Oklahoma City is bombed.

1995: Andy Summers's *Synaesthesia* is released.

June 1995: *The Police Live!* is released. This excellent double album features performances from 1979 and 1983.

World and Cultural Events

Sting, Andy Summers, and Stewart Copeland's Lives and Careers

February 1996: World chess champion, Garry Kasparov, loses a game to the chess computer "Deep Blue" for the first time. In 2000, Sting and four bandmates will lose to Kasparov within fifty minutes.

March 1996: Sting's *Mercury Falling* debuts. It features "I'm So Happy I Can't Stop Crying," which would be a hit for Toby Keith in late 1997.

July 1997: Gianni Versace is killed outside his home in Miami, Florida, by Andrew Cunanan. Sting will attend his memorial in Milan.

August 1997: Princess Diana is killed in a car accident.

August 1997: *Strontium 90: Police Academy* is released. This album features a performance in Paris on May 28, 1977, of Mike Howlett, Copeland, Sting, and Summers, collectively known as Strontium 90. This was the first time that Summers had performed with Sting and Copeland. After this concert, they changed their name to the Elevators, but after a couple more performances, they disbanded.

May 1998: Bear Grylls becomes the youngest British climber to scale Mount Everest at twenty-three.

World and Cultural Events	Sting, Andy Summers, and Stewart Copeland's Lives and Careers
	September 1998: *Spyro the Dragon* is released, featuring music from Stewart Copeland.
April 1999: Twelve students and a teacher are murdered at Columbine High School in Littleton, Colorado.	
	May 1999: Andy Summers's tribute to Thelonious Monk, *Green Chimneys: The Music of Thelonious Monk*, debuts.
	September 1999: Sting's *Brand New Day* is released. With the help of a Jaguar commercial, "Desert Rose" becomes a worldwide hit.
	May 2000: Stewart Copeland performs with Oysterhead at the New Orleans Jazz & Heritage Festival. He has to adjust to the improvisational nature of the group.
	September 2000: Andy Summers's tribute to Charles Mingus, *Peggy's Blue Skylight*, debuts.
October 2000: The USS *Cole* is damaged by terrorists.	
February 2001: U2 wins a Grammy Award for Song of the Year for "Beautiful Day."	

World and Cultural Events	*Sting, Andy Summers, and Stewart Copeland's Lives and Careers*
September 2001: New York City's World Trade Center and the Pentagon are attacked by the Al-Qaeda terrorist organization on September 11. A fourth hijacked plane crashes outside of Pittsburgh. A live performance by Sting takes place that same evening. He dedicates the resulting album to the victims of the attacks.	
	October 2001: Oysterhead's *The Grand Pecking Order* debuts.
November 2002: George W. Bush signs the Homeland Security Act, establishing the Department of Homeland Security.	
March 2003: Britain and the United States invade Iraq.	**March 2003**: The Police are inducted into the Rock and Roll Hall of Fame.
	August 2003: Copeland performs at La Notte della Taranta Festival.
	September 2003: Sting's *Sacred Love* debuts. Sting will look toward other musical challenges after this album is released.
	October 2003: Sting publishes his autobiography, *Broken Music*. Although he avoids discussing his time with The Police, reviews are positive.
December 2003: American troops capture Saddam Hussein.	

World and Cultural Events	*Sting, Andy Summers, and Stewart Copeland's Lives and Careers*
February 2004: Justin Timberlake rips off the bodice of Janet Jackson's costume during the halftime show of Super Bowl XXXVIII. Sting and No Doubt had performed at the Super Bowl halftime show the previous year.	
	March 2004: Summers's *Earth + Sky* debuts.
April 2005: Benedict XVI becomes the pope after the death of John Paul II.	
	June 2005: Copeland releases the CD/DVD version of *Orchestralli*, a live version of his chamber music.
August 2005: Hurricane Katrina destroys parts of the Gulf Coast and New Orleans.	
February 2006: Another punk trio, Green Day, wins a Grammy Award for Record of the Year for "Boulevard of Broken Dreams."	**September 2006**: Stewart Copeland's *Everyone Stares: The Police Inside Out* is released on DVD. Copeland had filmed much of the behind-the-scenes action of The Police on tour. The documentary details the energy and chaos surrounding the group.
	October 2006: Andy Summers's autobiography, *One Train Later*, is released to positive reviews. Summers's pre-Police stories are particularly amusing.

World and Cultural Events	*Sting, Andy Summers, and Stewart Copeland's Lives and Careers*
	October 2006: Sting's Renaissance album, *Songs from the Labyrinth*, debuts. Sting sings songs written by the Renaissance lutenist/songwriter, John Dowland.
	May 2007: The Police reunite and begin a record-breaking world tour.
June 2007: Tony Blair is replaced by Gordon Brown as prime minister of Great Britain.	
	August 2007: Summers's album with Ben Verdery, *First You Build a Cloud,* debuts. Also, an excellent compilation of Copeland's work, *The Stewart Copeland Anthology*, is released.
	March 2008: Copeland premieres his orchestral work, "Celeste," in Savannah, Georgia.
November 2008: Barack Obama is elected the 44th president of the United States.	**November 2008**: *Certifiable: Live from Buenos Aires*, live recordings from The Police's reunion tour, is released.
	July 2009: Sting publishes a collection of his lyrics, aptly titled *Lyrics by Sting*. Short backgrounds are offered, and the lyrics are presented in a remarkably elegant way.

World and Cultural Events

Sting, Andy Summers, and Stewart Copeland's Lives and Careers

October 2009: Sting's collection of folk tunes, *If on a Winter's Night . . .* , is released. Sting's interest in winter is integrated throughout the album.

January 2010: Stewart Copeland's autobiography, *Strange Things Happen*, debuts. This autobiography is more a collection of amusing stories than a full-fledged narrative of Copeland's life.

April 2010: An explosion on a British Petroleum platform off the coast of Louisiana kills eleven people and releases millions of gallons of crude oil into the Gulf of Mexico, making it the world's largest oil spill of its kind.

August 2010: Sting's orchestral album, *Symphonicities*, debuts. The orchestral arrangements provide an air of sophistication to Sting's pop compositions.

October 2010: A capsule is used to free the first of thirty-three Chilean miners trapped over a half mile underground. All the miners would be freed within twenty-four hours.

February 2011: Copeland debuts "Gamelan D'Drum" with the Dallas Symphony Orchestra.

World and Cultural Events

Sting, Andy Summers, and Stewart Copeland's Lives and Careers

March 2011: Japan is hit by a large earthquake, triggering a tsunami. The resulting tidal surge will destroy a series of nuclear reactors at the Fukushima Daiichi Nuclear Power Station.

April 2011: Prince William and Kate Middleton marry at Westminster Abbey in London.

May 2011: Osama bin Laden is killed in Abbottabad, Pakistan, by U.S. troops.

August 2011: Copeland participates in David Letterman's "Drum Solo Week." Drum aficionados are thrilled to hear Copeland perform a rare drum solo.

September 2012: Summers's Brazilian-inspired album *Fundamental* with Fernanda Takai debuts.

October 2012: Hurricane Sandy strikes New Jersey, New York, and Connecticut, making it the second costliest hurricane in the United States.

December 2012: Adam Lanza kills twenty-six people, including twenty children, at Sandy Hook Elementary School in Newtown, Connecticut.

World and Cultural Events	*Sting, Andy Summers, and Stewart Copeland's Lives and Careers*
February 2013: Pope Benedict XVI retires, the first pope to do so since 1415.	
	September 2013: The soundtrack to Sting's Broadway show, *The Last Ship*, is released. It provides a musical narrative to Sting's youth.
February 2014: The Ebola epidemic in West Africa begins. Also, Sting and Paul Simon begin a world tour together.	
	March 2014: Summers's rock band, Circa Zero, debuts *Circus Hero*. Summers was inspired by the 2007 reunion to form a new rock band.
	June 2014: Copeland's percussion concerto, "Poltroons in Paradise," debuts in Liverpool.
	September 2014: Sting's *The Last Ship* premieres on Broadway.
	October 2014: Sting is nominated for solo induction into the Rock and Roll Hall of Fame.
	April 2015: *Dare to Drum*, a documentary featuring Copeland's work with the percussion ensemble D'Drum premieres in Dallas, Texas.

ACKNOWLEDGMENTS

Thanks to George and Sandra West for fostering a love of music in me from the beginning, and my brothers, Matthew and Andrew, who are always there for me. Thanks to my dear friends, Tim Murray and Stacey Ewing, who have been invaluable sources of inspiration and knowledge. The University of North Texas music library is one of the finest libraries in the world, and I am fortunate to have access to its resources and staff. Thanks to the impeccable editors and staff at Rowman & Littlefield who have diligently helped me with every aspect of this book. Lastly, and most importantly, I could never have finished this project without the endless patience and support of my wife, Janelle. She makes it all possible.

INTRODUCTION

I grew up in the small town of Stuart on the east coast of South Florida and quickly learned that every stereotype about Florida life was true. I spent most of my youth amongst the elderly, enjoying endless quantities of sun, sandy beaches, and afternoon rains. Given the average age of Floridians, I also spent a considerable amount of time at the local mall. Of course, our mall had the common storefronts for the 1980s: the Barrel of Fun (a video game arcade shaped like a barrel), a store that only sold jelly beans, a robot named FUBAR, and the Tape Deck, a store that specialized in cassettes. Being a youth of limited means but with musical aspirations, buying a cassette was an important event that required a blend of patience and instinct, but on one evening I needed neither. As I entered the Tape Deck, I saw *Every Breath You Take: The Singles*. After an in-depth analysis of what little information was available on the front and back of the cassette, I purchased it. Although I was aware of The Police, I had never seriously pursued their music. But as I listened to "Roxanne," "Invisible Sun," and "King of Pain," I instantly discovered a set of musical idols. Of course, I soon purchased the entire back catalog from *Outlandos d'Amour* to *Synchronicity* and discovered countless ways in which their songs "spoke to me."

By the early nineties, I was maturing as a jazz musician. I revered jazz legends like Miles Davis, Duke Ellington, and Wynton Kelly, but I held few popular musicians in such high regard. Of course, Sting was the exception. His bands featured respected contemporary jazz artists like Branford Marsalis, Darryl Jones, and most importantly, Kenny

Kirkland. As a keyboardist, I was obsessed with Kirkland's solo on "Bring on the Night/When the World Is Running Down, You Make the Best of What's Still Around." I spent countless hours learning that solo, note for note. Kirkland's timing and harmonic inventiveness, along with the excellent accompaniment from Sting's band, combined to form one of the finest piano solos in the history of popular music. Although Kirkland passed away in 1998, Sting's current keyboardists frequently incorporate a "nod" to Kirkland's iconic solo in their own performances. This kind of inside knowledge made Sting's music even more compelling. He wasn't just creating the pop hits of the day; he was composing meaningful songs that addressed complex emotional and political issues, all the while being fun to sing along with.

As I finished my undergraduate and graduate degrees in jazz studies, I followed the career of Sting. His personal and political awareness was the perfect accompaniment to my own experiences as a twenty-something jazz performer. In fact, Sting was one of the very few popular artists whom most jazz performers respected. Likewise in the nineties, as Sting matured with *Soul Cages* and *Mercury Falling*, I was also encountering new personal challenges as my love of music performance evolved into a career in musicology.

By 2007, Stewart Copeland, Andy Summers, and Sting had successful post-Police careers and appeared to have lasting animosity towards each other, so when The Police reunited it seemed like the impossible had become a reality. To celebrate the event, I asked friends to fly in from various parts of the country to attend the show with me. The entire event is an equally surreal and sweet memory. Today, I find myself returning to the music of Sting and The Police, not just for nostalgia's sake, but as a way to reassess my own maturity. In a way, Sting and The Police have been the soundtrack to the last twenty-five years of my life.

When I was given the opportunity to write this book, I approached it as a labor of love and respect for a band that has helped shape my personal and musical identity, but I did not want to write another biography. There are multiple biographies already available. Christopher Sandford's *Sting: Demolition Man* (1998), Wensley Clarkson's *A Tale in the Sting* (2003), James Berryman's *Sting and I* (2005), and Chris Campion's *Walking on the Moon, The Untold Story of The Police and the Rise of New Wave Rock* (2010) detail the chronology of Sting and The

Police. These books have their strengths and weaknesses, and taken as a whole, offer a substantial source of anecdotes, band facts, and chronology. Moreover, indispensable fan sites like Police Wiki (http://thepolicewiki.org/) provide extraordinarily detailed chronological information on nearly everyone affiliated with The Police. Added to this list are the compelling autobiographies by each member of The Police. Andy Summers's *One Train Later* (2006) is a fascinating read that provides invaluable information on Summers's pre-Police years as well as insight into the band's commercial peak. *Strange Things Happen* (2009), Stewart Copeland's autobiography, is a collection of puckish short stories spanning Copeland's childhood to The Police reunion. Sting's autobiography, *Broken Music* (2005), is the narrative of his youth up to the beginnings of The Police. Each autobiography should be mandatory reading for any Police fan. These texts provide ample chronological information, so what could a new book add to the conversation?

Sting and The Police: Walking in Their Footsteps is not a retelling of the wild antics of The Police. Nor is it an attempt to psychoanalyze the relationships between the bandmates, their families, or business associates. Far too often the dramatic events surrounding these artists have overshadowed the music itself, and spurious anecdotes and opinion have become "fact." *Walking in Their Footsteps* takes into account that Summers, Copeland, and Sting are complex artists who have been victims of media-generated inaccuracies and misquotes. *Walking in Their Footsteps* does not add to those inaccuracies. In fact, *every* quote of Copeland, Summers, and Sting used in *Walking in Their Footsteps* has been personally transcribed from audio/video recordings or taken from their respective autobiographies, albums, and documentaries. You will not find misquotes or quotes taken out of context. What you *will* find in *Walking in Their Footsteps* is a series of essays in rough chronological order that place Sting and The Police within larger cultural and musical contexts. This, I believe, is the most enlightening way to listen and learn about The Police. The music that these three musicians created, and continue to create, is a hybrid product of musical and cultural influences that span decades. Arguably, the most compelling aspect of The Police is that they were able to combine these disparate influences into marketable, mainstream music, which has remained viable for generations.

In chapter 1, "The Police and the Progressive Rock, Punk, and Reggae Styles," I examine the giant steps The Police took to make use of these three musical styles throughout their repertoire. In so doing, they created musical hybrids that featured not only these styles but many others. As a result, The Police never fully embraced any one style. Although they frequently signified elements of progressive rock, punk, and reggae in their music, they rarely embraced any style wholesale. This chapter details their relationships with these styles and how they formed them into a distinctive musical sound.

The intricacies of The Police's style hybrids are explored further in chapter 2, "The Police and the Style Mosaic." As a collection of large and small tiles, a mosaic is a good analogy for The Police's approach to the music, as the large "tiles" they used connote the most prevalent styles in their sound, and the smaller tiles represent hints of other styles incorporated into the whole. When all these tiles are combined, they form a complete tune or mosaic, but the individual parts remain identifiable. Songs like "Roxanne," "Message in a Bottle," and "Bring on the Night" are compelling examples of this phenomenon.

Chapter 3, "Sting and the Album Mosaic," details Sting's work as a solo artist. Sting did not create the same kinds of style mosaics as he did with The Police, but this is not to say that he was no longer interested in appropriating styles. On the contrary, Sting was more interested than ever in various musical styles, but many of his songs do not demonstrate the song-based mosaics composed by The Police. Instead, Sting creates album-based style mosaics that are equally compelling. Instead of individual songs, which feature a rich mosaic of integrated styles, Sting creates albums that are collections of songs written in various styles.

In chapter 4, "Selling The Police and Sting to the World," I discuss the non-musical connections between these artists and their listeners. Of course, the music of Sting and The Police is important, but the tours, music videos, marketing, and promotional videos contributed to establishing the now iconic images of these artists as well.

Many fans know Sting as an activist, and in chapter 5, "Sting in the Age of Global Activism," his connections to various charitable campaigns are discussed. Sting's personal involvement in global activism coincides with the rise of highly publicized campaigns in the 1980s. Sting was involved with Band Aid, Live Aid, and the Conspiracy of Hope and Human Rights Now! tours, as well as with his own Rainforest

Foundation. The stories and people behind these campaigns are remarkable.

Chapter 6, "The Police and the Rock Trio," provides a short history of rock's most influential trios. Although there are countless rock trios, only a few have achieved the highest levels of popularity and influence. This chapter places The Police within the historic narratives of Cream, The Jimi Hendrix Experience, Rush, Nirvana, and Green Day.

Lastly, chapter 7, "The Music after The Police," discusses the musical paths taken by Stewart Copeland, Andy Summers, and Sting after their band ended. Each musician has made uncommon musical choices, which have proven to be challenging. This chapter ends with a discussion of the musical legacy of The Police.

On a final note, this book is ultimately about placing the music of these artists in various contexts. Unlike much popular music, which can be remarkably shallow, the music of Copeland, Summers, and Sting stands up to in-depth analysis. And, in many ways, this music will reward you for doing so. Moreover, readers should *listen* and contemplate the music discussed in these chapters. Please take my views on these vast repertoires as an invitation to begin your own explorations. This music is worth it.

THE POLICE AND THE PROGRESSIVE ROCK, PUNK, AND REGGAE STYLES

In 2003, The Police were inducted into the Rock and Roll Hall of Fame, and the designated presenter that evening was the lead singer of No Doubt, Gwen Stefani. Stefani was understandably nervous. She had been a fan of The Police since she was a teenager, and induction is an honor for even the most jaded rock performers. During her speech, Stefani echoed many of the thoughts that fans of The Police have shared for decades. She described the era of The Police and their combative reputation: "It was the eighties. It was an amazing time to be growing up and be a music fan . . . even as a thirteen-year-old kid I was aware of the band's reputation for fighting and that Sting was a little bit scary." Stefani later described a concert that would ultimately change her musical life: "This was one of the most memorable concerts of my life. They played so many incredible songs, 'Wrapped around Your Finger,' 'King of Pain,' and, of course, 'Every Breath You Take.' This song was everywhere that summer. You couldn't get away from it . . . it was a life-changing performance for me."

Indeed, The Police and "Every Breath You Take" *were* everywhere in 1983. The ubiquitous song was the capstone to a phenomenally successful run that culminated in five Grammy awards (not including the award given in 1983 to Sting for "Every Breath You Take" for Song of the Year), millions of albums sold, and record-breaking world tours. Even the preface to *Rolling Stone*'s "Reader's Poll" of 1983 highlighted the popularity of The Police:

For *Rolling Stone* readers, music in 1983 meant two names—Michael Jackson and The Police. Between them, they walked away with seven first-place finishes in our Eighth Annual Readers' Poll: Jackson took top honors in the Artist of the Year, Soul Artist and Best Video categories, while The Police were winners in the Band of the Year, Album of the Year, Single of the Year and Songwriter of the Year divisions. ("Rolling Stone Music Awards," 18)

The Police and Sting earned more votes than popular music icons like U2, Talking Heads, Def Leppard, Billy Joel, Elvis Costello, and of course, Michael Jackson. Soon after, at the peak of their popularity, The Police went on a "hiatus" that lasted twenty-one years. Nevertheless, artists like Gwen Stefani held The Police in the highest regard and frequently cited the band as an important influence. At the induction ceremony, Stefani summed up her thoughts on the band: "The Police achieved something with me and many others that I believe is one of the most difficult and fulfilling accomplishments. They created music that inspired me to be in a band. They motivated me and many others to create and grab hold of our destiny."

How did a band that disbanded in 1984 compel contemporary pop music icons such as Gwen Stefani to state, "It was a life-changing performance"? A look at the diverse musical backgrounds of Andy Summers, Stewart Copeland, and Sting will help explain their lasting influence, but to do so requires exploring the pervasive musical styles of the 1970s and how these disparate styles were formed into a cohesive and identifiable musical expression. The early musical experiences of each band member are linked to three musical styles that were most prevalent within the band's repertoire: progressive rock, punk, and reggae.

The members of The Police were acutely aware of the intricacies and significance of style. Sting frequently railed against stylistic purity, once stating that popular music is at its best when it is an amalgamation of various stylistic practices and forms: "I believe pop music should be a great mongrel. In other words, it can take from any source, from classical music, from jazz, from literature, from history. All human endeavor can be included in pop music as far as I'm concerned. The critics will tell you, 'no it can't.' Sorry, they're wrong" (*Sting Unplugged*). Years later, Andy Summers echoed Sting's views on style:

> We weren't sitting around listening to lots of rock bands trying to be a heavy rock band. The information that we used to make our rock music came from several different sources. Both Sting and I are very eclectic. We're very much on the same page about a lot of things, obviously music. We both love Brazilian music, we both like classical guitar. We listen to Indian music, as well as blues and jazz. We can play all of these things actually . . . what made us interesting was *not* listening to rock bands, but sort of taking it from other stuff. (Summers interview)

The Police, especially in the early years, did not arbitrarily pick styles to integrate into their oeuvre; they chose musical styles which were familiar and accessible.

PROGRESSIVE ROCK

The first prevalent style that all three members of The Police were well versed in is commonly known as progressive rock, or "prog rock." Stewart Copeland, Andy Summers, and Sting had extensive professional experience in the prog rock style. Copeland's brother, Miles Copeland, was the manager of Wishbone Ash, Renaissance, and Climax Blues Band, all of which were part of the progessive movement. Through his brother's connections, Stewart Copeland became the manager and later the drummer for the venerable progessive rock band, Curved Air. Andy Summers's connections with progressive rock were even deeper than Copeland's. In 1967, Summers was a member of Dantalian's Chariot (a psychedelic version of Zoot Money's Big Roll Band), which was a quintessential psychedelic group of the day featuring a colorful stage show, bold album art, and theatrical lyrics. Just a year later, Summers joined the seminal progressive rock band, Soft Machine, and although Summers was part of the band for less than a year, he rated this as a pivotal musical experience:

> We begin rehearsing and I fit my guitar into their music. In its best moments the music of the Soft Machine at this time is a swirling rush of dense, washy keyboards, repeated vocal lines, and drum patterns that fall outside any traditional song formats. In the vernacular of the moment, it would be called "trippy." (*One Train Later*, 115)

The "washy keyboards" and "drum patterns that fall outside any traditional song formats" are characteristics very similar to those of the progressive rock style. To a lesser extent, Sting's early professional experiences were also tied to progressive rock. In late 1974, Sting began rehearsing with Last Exit, a band inspired by the jazz-fusion band, Return to Forever. While the members of Last Exit leaned more towards jazz and funk than rock, their performances displayed instrumental virtuosity and literary themes that were clearly influenced by the prevalent sounds of the progressive rock movement.

Progressive rock is a substyle of rock that originated and evolved largely in England and Europe between approximately 1968 and 1976, and although the popularity of progressive rock was in decline by the time The Police formed in 1977, its influence is found throughout The Police's repertoire. As with all styles of music, there are musical and extramusical traits with which it is commonly associated. Progessive rock is routinely characterized by the use of instrumental and vocal virtuosity (yes, "Awaken"), surrealistic themes (King Crimson, "Moonchild," including "The Dream" and "The Illusion"), and instrumentals (Mike Oldfield, "Tubular Bells"). All of these elements are found within the work of The Police.

In terms of virtuosity or musical "chops," The Police rarely used instrumental mastery as an end unto itself. In most cases, they utilized technical ability as a means to create vibrant pop songs, but each member at times demonstrates technical mastery throughout their repertoire. In the case of Sting, there are moments when his bass playing displays the accuracy, lightness, and rhythmic unpredictably of the finest bassists of the era. For instance, "Deathwish," released on the 1979 album *Reggatta de Blanc*, is a two-part form featuring the familiar "Bo Diddley" groove in the first verse and a more typical rock groove in the chorus. The bass line of the verse is somewhat simple; it consists of only one repeated pitch. In the chorus, though, Sting creates an agile repeated pattern that not only displays his instrumental acumen but also demarcates the form of the entire tune, ultimately making this simple song noteworthy. Along similar lines, the bass parts to "No Time This Time" (*Reggatta de Blanc*) and "Rehumanize Yourself" (*Ghost in the Machine*) demonstrate that Sting's technical skills were a step beyond the typical rock bassist's skill level. Not only did Sting display his skill through nimble technique, but he also created bass lines that featured unusual musical phrasing. For instance, the bass part to "Walking on the Moon" (*Reggatta de Blanc*), besides being one of the most recognizable bass lines in pop music history, is deceptively difficult to perform. At the beginning of the tune Sting lays down the initial groove by playing a typical reggae rolling bass line, but when his vocals enter, the bass line acts as an instrumental response to each line of lyrics. A closer listening reveals that the call-and-response roles of the bass and vocals are not absolute; rather, the lines elide at times, creating a nuanced relationship between bass and voice.

As with Sting, Andy Summers's technical mastery cannot be solely defined by how fast he can play, although his years of professional experience did provide him with ample technical firepower. Summers did not typically take long guitar solos while with The Police. The band eschewed overly long demonstrations of technical bravura and purposely distilled their music into the widely accepted pop format of four-minute songs featuring a chorus, verse, and possibly a short guitar solo. There was simply no time for extended instrumental solos. Despite the compact nature of the pop format, Summers recorded a handful of short but memorable solos. For instance, at the midpoint of the pseudo-punk-styled song "Peanuts" (*Outlandos d'Amour*), Summers performs a fast, loud, and commanding guitar solo, during which he clearly channels the youthful aggression of punk, a movement with which The Police had somewhat reluctantly affiliated themselves. Although Summers conveys the energy of punk, he does not use its typical musical vocabulary. His repeated use of atonal passages echoes the musical vocabulary of 1960s psychedelia, a generation of music that he grew up with and which is historically connected to progressive rock but not punk. Possibly the finest example of Summers's technique is found midway through "Flexible Strategies," a B-side instrumental from *Ghost in the Machine*, where he overlays atonality and non-Western scales onto the rhythm-and-blues (R&B) groove of the tune. This is an unusual choice. Summers was well versed in the R&B musical vocabulary, and he certainly could have performed a more typical guitar solo that employed more traditional phrasings and patterns, but like his bandmates, Summers was more interested in combining disparate styles and sounds than rehashing musical traditions.

Perhaps the performer who was the most overtly virtuosic was Stewart Copeland. His youthfully energetic and innovative approach to drumming made him arguably the most vibrant musical force of the group. Copeland's insistent yet graceful drumming style is apparent throughout The Police's relatively short life span. Of course, there is more to the art of drumming than just being a powerful and energetic timekeeper; good drummers are also musical directors and orchestrators. This may seem like an unusual statement, but a good drummer can shape and delineate various parts of a song by "orchestrating." For example, a verse can be emphasized by a skipping hi-hat groove, later the chorus may feature a heavy backbeat/snare drum groove that includes a ride cymbal, and then the bridge may include a tom-tom pattern. These are not arbitrary choices, and professional drummers consider these various alternatives very carefully. Moreover an elite drummer like Stewart Copeland seamlessly transitions from one groove to the next, virtually making the drum part a composition unto itself.

Considering the progressive rock backgrounds of each of the three musicians, it is no wonder that they were technically skilled. Sting humbly sums up their approach to technique: "We were a good band, and people responded to us on a musical level. Not necessarily a fashion level or a cultural level, just a musical level. We were a little group, and we could really play, and we had some good songs" (Bendjelloul).

Literary surrealism was another important element of the progressive rock aesthetic, and The Police evoked a similarly surrealistic approach to their lyrics. For instance, Sting used both T. S. Eliot and Hermann Hesse as inspiration for Police songs. For example, he lifts the second line from Eliot's "The Love Song of J. Alfred Prufrock," "When the evening is spread out against the sky," for use as the second line in his own creation, "Bring on the Night." Sting also found inspiration in Hermann Hesse's idea that all feelings and experiences, however joyful or tragic, are a part of the cyclical unity of nature. This philosophical approach to life would be an important inspiration to Sting's post-Police career, but he created a narrative of surrealistic social commentary within a handful of Police songs as well. For example, in "Synchronicity II," Sting uses a metaphor involving an overworked father and a creature rising from a Scottish lake. Sting paints a bleak picture of a factory worker who "doesn't think to wonder why" and who, along with his compatriots, is "packed like lemmings into shiny metal boxes." Meanwhile, an unknown creature is crawling to the surface of a dark Scottish lake. Through this surrealistic metaphor, Sting comments on the personal and professional alienation that can occur in a modern industrial society. In "Synchronicity II," alienation ultimately creates a monster, which lurks within the husband as a "shadow on the door." The rest of the band is in tune with this imagery as well, with Summers's howling guitar, laser-like keyboard shrieks, and Copeland's manic drumming in the background.

The final characteristic that The Police borrowed from the progressive era is an interest in instrumentals. Again, the progressive era was predicated on performance ability, and this frequently resulted in demonstrations of instrumental virtuosity. Instrumental tracks were frequently included on prog rock albums like Emerson, Lake & Palmer's "The Barbarian," King Crimson's "Larks' Tongues in Aspic (Part 1)," The Alan Parsons Project's "Lucifer," and Rush's "YYZ." These instrumentals demonstrated that these bands offered more than mere pop songs; these were "real" musicians who did not need the crutch of lyrics to convey emotions and narrative. The Police, though, did not relegate their instrumental tracks to blatant virtuosic demonstrations. They released six instrumental tracks throughout their career, ranging from the Grammy Award–winning "Reggatta de Blanc" and "Behind My Camel" to simple B-sides and album fillers like "Flexible Strategies." Some of these tracks, like "Behind My Camel" and "Shambelle," were musical experiments written by Andy Summers, and they represent his more avant-garde approach to composition. The brooding "Behind My Camel" incorporates swirls of guitar synthesizer with an angular and menacing melody, while "Shambelle" represents Summers's harmonic mastery. During "Shambelle," the repetitive bass line is uninteresting, but Summers superimposes continually moving harmonies that are quite sophisticated and foretell his later interest in sonic imagery, while other tunes represent the seemingly effortless ability of The Police to write captivating pop music. Pieces like "Reggatta de Blanc," "Masoko Tanga," "The Other Way of Stopping," and "Flexible Strategies," appear to be somewhat unfinished, but with added lyrics and some further production, they surely could have been hits. These tracks seem to state, "our throwaway tracks would be anyone else's hits."

Despite their many prog rock leanings, it is important to note that The Police should not be classified as a progressive rock band. In fact, The Police defied being classified as *any* one kind of band. Summers, Copeland, and Sting deftly used distinctive stylistic elements from the era to create a "band sound." Although there are clear instances of the progressive rock style in their repertoire, the majority of their work does not evoke the most common characteristics of that era. The same can be said for The Police's use of the next prevalent style, punk rock.

PUNK ROCK

The precise origins of punk are difficult to pinpoint. Some commentators espouse that punk evolved from underground American bands like the Velvet Underground, New York Dolls, and The Stooges, and those influences eventually reached England. Indeed, each of these bands are frequently labeled as contributors to the punk aesthetic. The avant-garde experimentation of the Velvet Underground influenced punk as well as other styles of popular music of the 1970s. The New York Dolls' visual style and hints of androgyny influenced not only the leather-clad punks but the new wave movement of the 1980s as well. And certainly, the sheer musical energy and social commentary of Iggy Pop (along with The Stooges) directly influenced the punk artists of the later 1970s. This underground musical movement ultimately converged at a New York City nightclub called CBGB, and inspired the formation of arguably the first true American punk band, The Ramones. The Ramones admit that they were a result of this underground movement: "We took the rock sound into a psychotic world and narrowed it down into a straight line of energy. In an era of progressive rock, with its complexities and counterpoints, we had a perspective of non-musicality and intelligence that took over from musicianship" (Laing, 23). Along with other punk bands like Suicide, Television, and the Voidoids, The Ramones heavily influenced the British punk rock movement. The other punk origin story, though, focuses more on English punk rock as a working-class youth movement galvanized by discontent with unemployment, racial tensions, and an economic recession, and not necessarily a child of American punk. The British version of punk was more political, angrier, and garnered much more media attention. Unlike the American punk movement, which remained largely underground, British rockers gained national noteriety very quickly through the controversial actions of the most prominent English punk band, the Sex Pistols. Admittedly, the Sex Pistols were influenced by the American punk movement, but they ultimately became the face of punk. Both punk narratives are valid, and the truth is probably somewhere in between.

The Police did not adopt the aesthetics of punk rock wholesale; rather, they recontextualized many punk characteristics by combining them with other style signifiers. The Police's fortuitous formation in London in 1977 enabled them to maximize their exposure to punk rock, which resulted in their first two albums, *Outlandos d'Amour* and *Reggatta de Blanc*, borrowing heavily from the punk style. The three band members recognized that the punk movement was an exciting and vital time in popular music: "It was a great time in music, 1976 to '77, because the punk thing happened in London. Things were very wide open. People were ready to listen, so it was a very good time to be starting a new band," Andy Summers recalls (*Outlandos to Synchonicities*). Indeed, The Police connected with the raw, youthful energy of punk, and in many ways, they were at the center of this new music era.

Although The Police were unquestionably part of English punk culture, their music and musicianship never fully fit in. Stewart Copeland comments, "We were real musicians and we had to hide that . . . we had very strict rules in The Police. Because we were a punk band, we had to cut our hair. The songs had to be political and they had to be very concise, very short, very simple, very stark" (Cinequest Film Festival). Indeed, one of the most defining aspects of punk music was its amateurism, but The Police were "serious musicians." In fact, punk culture publically embraced its "do-it-yourself" credo. For example, in a 1976 issue of the punk fanzine, *Sideburns*, a simplistic drawing of a guitar fret board accompanies the statement, "This is a chord. This is another. This is a third. Now form a band" (Savage, 280). The punk community was proud of its amateurism, but The Police were simply too experienced and talented to fit into the punk DIY ethos. Early on, Henry Padovani, the first guitarist of The Police, recognized the problems they had assimilating into punk culture:

> The Police at the time, at the end of '77 and '78, were not a band for an audience that existed in London. They were experimenting with reggae, with a different kind of attitude . . . the band that was left was Stewart from Curved Air, Sting from Last Exit, a jazz-rock band from Newcastle, and Andy Summers, older than anybody in town who played with Kevin Ayers and all those guys. How uncool do you want

to be? In the eyes of the enemy, it was the worst band in England. Nobody liked The Police. (*Rock Milestones*)

Nevertheless, aspects of punk's amateurism found their way into The Police repertoire.

"Roxanne," recorded in early 1978 and released on *Outlandos d'Amour*, provides a glimpse into how The Police incorporated the impression of DIY into some of their earlier work. In the introduction of "Roxanne," a dissonant piano chord sounds, and Sting laughs in response. During the recording of the vocal track, Sting evidently backs into a piano (indicating just how small the studio was), bumps the keys and laughs. This was a low-budget recording, and even the producer, Nigel Gray, admits that there were certain studio limitations: "I remember recording 'Roxanne,' because I had to actually conduct it. We never used click tracks and time codes and that kind of thing in those days, because they didn't exist, so I had to go out into the studio and stand on one of the loudspeakers so they could all see me" (Campion, 57). Of course, this kind of mistake could have been easily remedied by either editing the mistake out of the track or by simply starting over. Instead, The Police decided to leave it in. Although the piano and laugh were easily fixed mistakes, The Police evoked the punk DIY aesthetic by implying that it was a random and spontaneous occurrence. Another instance of DIY in "Roxanne" occurs during the first chorus (approximately one minute into the tune). The lyrics of this chorus only consist of "Roxanne. Put on the red light." The word "Roxanne" is sung by harmonized background vocals, and Sting responds with "put on the red light." All three members of the band could be singing the harmonized "Roxanne," and they sound jagged, barely in tune, and sloppy. Keep in mind that Sting had a good ear for harmonies and background vocals. On other *Outlandos* tracks, such as "Next to You" and "Truth Hits Everybody," the background vocals are well constructed, but not in "Roxanne." During the editing process, The Police wisely chose to leave these flawed vocals in the recording. This decision lent an air of amateurism to the recording, helping to create the raw excitement that made "Roxanne" so popular.

"Dead End Job" is a fine example of how The Police periodically co-opted the sentiments of the punk generation through lyrics, especially in the early years. "Dead End Job" was originally recorded in August

1977, a period when The Police were most influenced by the punk aesthetic and while Henry Padovani, the punk guitarist, was still in the group. The most recognizable version, after Andy Summers had replaced Padovani, was recorded in early 1978. The tune begins with a DIY reading of working-class job ads; soon after, Copeland kicks off a furious tempo accompanied by Sting's articulate and driving bass line. Although the energy and shuffle-like groove is reminiscent of punk groups like The Damned, the musicianship is so outstanding that a punk aficionado would certainly note the absence of typical punk musical amateurism. Nevertheless, Sting begins with the line, "I don't want no dead end job," then continues with an anti-establishment narrative throughout the tune with lines like, "Don't wanna be no teacher, I don't wanna be no slave," and "The queue gets longer every day, I just ain't got time to stay." Sting performs these lyrics using a growling vocal timbre, recalling the most famous punk vocalist of the day, Johnny Rotten. Even with the anti-establishment lyrics and the punkish vocal timbre, The Police do not adopt the punk aesthetic in its entirety, but as "Dead End Job" ends, the punk signifiers become more pronounced. Sting screams in frustration, "Awwww, you got me pissed off with this dead end shit," and Summers begins reading from the employment ads again. The tune comes to a crashing close, fueled by punk-inspired frustration.

Of course, The Police never proclaimed to be a punk band. They only used punk as a single element of their group sound, but listeners, as they typically do, needed to place them in a category, and punk was as good as any. But when The Police were classified and compared to their punk contemporaries, their music rarely fulfilled listeners' expectations. As most punk fans had little patience for inauthenticity, The Police were typically labeled "peroxide pretenders." It should be noted that the music of The Police was a product of the era and the musical environment in which they existed. In some ways, their sound was created more from communal instinct than from careful planning. Andy Summers states, "When we came together, forming the sound of the group, we never really scratched our heads to look for something different or tried to be different. It was all completely instinctive" (*Outlandos to Synchonicities*). These same instincts led The Police to their most distinctive style, reggae.

REGGAE

Reggae might be the most identifiable style associated with The Police; after all, they named their second album *Reggatta de Blanc*. But to many listeners, reggae and Jamaica are synonymous. Moreover, reggae embodies not only the popular view of Jamaica, but the spirituality of many Jamaicans as well. Noted Jamaican performer Alton Ellis attempted to define the importance of reggae to Jamaicans: "I hope Jamaicans don't ever forget that reggae is a culture. It's not just a music, it's a culture belonging to us, created by us, and we must take care of it" (O'Brien Chang, v). It was no small matter for The Police to co-opt aspects of this vital music, and at times they were criticized for it. The Police utilized certain elements of reggae, just as they did with punk, progressive rock, and many other musical styles, and integrated them into their sound. They never adopted all aspects of reggae and never proclaimed themselves a "reggae band." But The Police *did* use the inherent musical space and relaxed attitude found in reggae to counter the dense and manic sounds of punk.

The Police were aware of the dialogues surrounding their musical choices, and they frequently articulated their positions on style. In 1979, Sting addressed their use of reggae styles:

> As a white, English group we have an advantage over black, Jamaican groups playing reggae. Because it's not our music, we can bring something else to it, so we adapt a foreign music to our own needs, and what comes out is totally different. We could adapt, say, Swedish folk music to our particular music, and we'd get something different from Swedes. It's that kind of interesting combination of two factors. (Interview, Swedish Television)

In this statement lies the essence of how The Police assimilated multiple musical styles; they "adapt a foreign music" to their needs, and what is produced is "totally different." Stewart Copeland, though, was a bit more contentious when commenting on style appropriation:

> When different cultures rub up against each other creative sparks fly. That's always been the same through history and music. For instance, the fact that, in my opinion, the best kind of rock and roll has been English rock and roll. Even though it comes from American

sources, from the American blacks is where it comes from, from blues and everything, still all the best rock and roll bands in the past have all been English, The Who, Stones, Beatles, the list goes on forever. There's no corresponding list of American greats. (Interview, Swedish Television)

Indeed, when cultures come in contact, musical hybrids can result, and the history of Jamaican and British musical cultures "rubbing against each other" is particularly important in understanding The Police and reggae.

The distinctive sound of reggae is the result of a combination of musical characteristics. To begin with, reggae is nearly always in a quadruple meter. This is because the interlocking rhythms essential to reggae do not work well in triple or odd meters. These interlocking rhythms are the responsibility of every member of the group. For instance, the guitar plays an important role in reggae in providing the important "skank" musical figure, which occurs on each up beat. If one counts a reggae tune as 1 *and* 2 *and* 3 *and* 4 *and*, then the skank occurs during the "ands." Moreover, the guitar usually performs this skank pattern in a scratchy or choppy fashion, almost imitating a percussion instrument. To many listeners, the skank is the most identifiable aspect of reggae, and Andy Summers dutifully played this pattern in many Police songs. Drums also are an important component of reggae, and there are typically three basic drum patterns used: one drop, rockers, and steppers. Once again, if one counts reggae as 1 *and* 2 *and* 3 *and* 4 *and*, the one-drop pattern features an accent on beat 3. There is no accent on beat 1, so beat 1 is dropped, thus the term "one drop." This accent is usually made either by the bass drum with a snare hit or cross stick. The rockers pattern is very similar to the one drop, only in this case beat 1 is not "dropped" but can be performed using a variety of hi-hat patterns, cross sticks, snare hits, or cymbal crashes. Lastly, the steppers pattern utilizes a bass drum pulse on all four beats, enabling the drummer to ornament the pattern with hi hats, cymbals, or snare drum patterns. Stewart Copeland was familiar with these three patterns, and they were all an integral part of his drumming style. The electric bass plays a significant role in reggae as well. Most listeners agree that the dark and repetitive nature of reggae bass lines are essential to reggae's danceable nature. More importantly, many reggae bass lines form a countermelody to the vocal line. Certainly, this countermelody is not as apparent as the vocal line, but when the two melodies are synchronized, they can create that unique, "floating" feel. For instance, the bass and vocal lines in "Walking on the Moon" are entirely different, yet they complement each other and create an impression of lightness.

The influence of reggae on Copeland, Summers, and Sting is a result of reggae's unique position in English society. The obvious political connections between the two cultures extend from the colonial past of Jamaica to its eventual independence in 1962, but there were musical ties between Great Britain and Jamaica as well. In the 1950s, companies like Melodisc imported records from the West Indies that featured cover versions of American R&B songs. By the 1960s, record labels like Bluebeat, Orbitone, and Planitone imported more distinctly Jamaican music into England. By the late 1960s, reggae influences began appearing in English and American pop culture. By the mid-1970s, mainstream artists like Paul Simon ("Mother and Child Reunion"), Three Dog Night ("Black and White"), Stevie Wonder ("Boogie On Reggae Woman"), and Eric Clapton ("I Shot the Sheriff") had integrated reggae elements into some of their music. During this period, the music businessman and producer Chris Blackwell successfully marketed Bob Marley as an international reggae star. Marley's music was frequently tinged with joyful melodies and sunny rhythms, though his lyrics were often political and rebellious. Songs like "Get Up, Stand Up," "Slave Driver," Babylon System," and "Africa Unite" were powerful statements to the underclasses in both Jamaica and Great Britain.

By the late 1970s, the English punk movement had co-opted not only some of the musical characteristics of reggae but its revolutionary narratives as well. Punk artists like The Clash ("Police and Thieves"), The Slits ("Instant Hit"), and Elvis Costello ("Watching the Detectives") incorporated reggae elements into some of their music. Young punks and Rasta youth held a shared antagonism towards authority for good reason; both communities were victims of police brutality. In 1977, reggae DJ Don Letts shared a personal account of his encounters with authority:

> 'Cause like, Johnny Rotten was telling me the other day. He's walkin' down the street now and the cops are hittin' on him. Takin' him in the van, tryin' to bust him for this and that. 'Cause of the way he looks . . . it's the same shit we go through. Like, with me hair and the red, gold and green. Copper stopped me in me car and tell me I

should walk, cops actually told me I should walk. (Letts, "Black-White," 8)

It is impossible to know precisely how or when The Police were introduced to reggae. Copeland has stated that one of the first instances when he analyzed a drumming style was while listening to Bob Marley in college. Some say that Sting threw a New Year's Eve party in 1977 using Copeland's reggae records and was interested in the music from that point forward. At any rate, reggae recordings were clearly available to discerning listeners, which The Police surely were, but one source of reggae was likely available to all members of the group. In January 1977, Don Letts became the official DJ of the punk mecca, the Roxy in London. Rastafarian Letts, who was born and raised in London, had been managing a trendy clothing store named Acme Attractions and was known to play reggae records in the shop. This unique musical reputation led to his employment at the Roxy. Letts comments on his choice of music at the Roxy:

> The Roxy was started by Andrew Czezowski as a direct response to an emerging scene that already had a new soundtrack and new attitude but no place to play. Andrew was aware of the buzz created by the music I was playing in the shop, so he asked me to DJ there on a regular basis, and I hesitantly took the job. It meant I was perfectly placed to witness the most exciting and inspiring period of my life. There were no UK punk records to play because none had been made yet. In between the fast and the furious punk sets, I played dub reggae, although I did spin some MC5, Ramones, Stooges and New York Dolls. (Letts, London interview)

Keep in mind that The Police were hungry for musical connections and inspiration in early 1977, and they frequently visited the Roxy. In fact, The Police even performed at the Roxy at various times during the spring and summer of 1977.

During the alternations of reggae and punk at the Roxy, Don Letts noticed an interesting phenomenon; the punk music that was played energized the crowd while the reggae relaxed them. Letts describes this musical alternation and its connection to drug use: "Speed was usually the drug of choice while listening to the Detroit garage bands, but once the heavy bass dropped on a Prince Far I track like "Under Heavy

Manners," spliffs were definitely the order of the day" (London interview). Letts recognized that mixing the aggression of punk with the relaxed groove of reggae created a compelling musical sensibility. The members of The Police may have sensed the same potential and subsequently created songs mixing the energy of rock with the laid-back feel of reggae, imitating, in a way, the alternations that were played at venues like the Roxy.

The basic nature of reggae provides an ambient musical environment that highlights groove over all else. The bass and vocal countermelodies, along with the uncluttered one-drop drum pattern and guitar skank, naturally create brief moments of silence that most musicians know as "musical space." The musical textures created by Peter Tosh, Burning Spear, Bob Marley, or Max Romeo are not dense like those of rock, progressive rock, or punk. These artists avoided filling in music spaces with roaring guitars, drum fills, and thumping bass lines. They created textures that "breathed." The members of The Police were particularly interested in musical space as well. Sting elaborates on silence and space:

> The perfect music is probably silence, and that as musicians all we really do is create a wonderful frame around that perfection which is silence. The beginning of Beethoven's Fifth Symphony begins with one beat of silence. It doesn't start on "one." One of my greatest teachers was Miles Davis. Everything he didn't play was as eloquent as the things he did play. Leaving space. (Pozner)

Andy Summers was also interested in musical space:

> I tend to like very spare, clean situations with a lot of clarity. I've always thought clarity is a very earthy quality. It moves people. I think in the case of The Police, the simplicity and the openness of the three-piece sound is an exciting quality . . . it excites people. Maybe they don't know, but I think it's the clarity. (Interview, French journalist)

Even on their debut album, *Outlandos d'Amour*, The Police frequently used clarity and space as a counterbalance to the more dense and busy sounds of rock.

"So Lonely" is on the second track of side one of *Outlandos d'Amour*, so it is likely the first example many listeners heard of The

Police's reggae/rock hybrid. On the surface, The Police use reggae and rock in a relatively simplistic manner. The verses are in reggae style, and the choruses are a fast, punkish rock. During the first half of "So Lonely," the verse (reggae) and chorus (rock) alternate. The verses are created using the reggae one-drop drum pattern and a very typical bass line. Although Summers initially plays the guitar skank, he does not slavishly stick to it. At various times he percussively hits the skank, but at others he slurs the pattern, and sometimes he abandons the skank altogether and provides slippery fills. While Summers was certainly a good enough performer to imitate any reggae pattern he chose, in this case, he decided on a relatively loose interpretation of the skank. This indicates that even at this early stage of their careers The Police rarely adopted any style wholesale. This reggae texture is transparent and somewhat fragile. In fact, it perfectly frames the lyrics that reflect the same feelings, "I can only play that part and sit and nurse my broken heart." The rock choruses abruptly push the fragile verses out of the way with the chant of "so lonely," accompanied by a pulsing bass line and a thrashing drum pattern. At the midpoint of "So Lonely," Summers begins his guitar solo over the one-drop pattern, agile bass line, and guitar skank of the verses. Initially, this texture is nearly identical to any of the prior verses, but at the midpoint of Summers's solo, Sting and Copeland launch into a rock texture, while the guitar skank remains unchanged. At this precise moment, The Police create a true hybrid between rock and reggae. Following the guitar solo and another chorus, the reggae texture reappears, but this time the dense chorus dissipates into a thin reggae texture, providing so much musical space that Sting is free to cut away from the lyrics to riff on the word "lonely." This mood change is more daring than it appears. Most pop groups are reluctant to move abruptly from a high-energy and driving chorus to a low-energy, transparent texture, but the musical space that The Police create here has an energy unto itself. There are no thrashing cymbals or guitar power chords, but there is still plenty of musical energy. What The Police create at this moment is a sense of suspense through musical space. All three musicians tiptoe across the delicate underlying reggae pulse, providing the listener with the sense that a musical payoff will come. Of course, The Police soon provide that payoff with a roaring final presentation of the chorus. During live performances, The Police accentuate this suspense by elongating this section of "So Lonely," using it as a moment in which they can invite the audience to participate or simply as a break for the hard-working trio. "So Lonely" is an early example of these Police hybrids, and they continued this formula later in their career as well.

"Wrapped around Your Finger" is one of the most popular tunes ever recorded by The Police. It was recorded in early 1983, and by then The Police had matured to a point where stylistic references were now more subtle and sophisticated but no less important. Part of the allure of "Wrapped around Your Finger" is the combination of literary references framed by the now familiar hybrid texture of reggae and rock styles. Unlike prior examples of this mixing, this time, The Police only allude to reggae. The reggae texture still provides Sting with the space to perform his narrative, but now the sunny deposition of reggae is swept aside by a more foreboding sound. During the introduction, there is no familiar skank pattern; instead, there is a series of chime-like sounds supported by a murky reggae bass line, while Copeland cleverly alludes to the one-drop drum pattern without fully realizing it. The texture of the introduction melts into the first verse, which begins Sting's sophisticated narrative.

"Wrapped around Your Finger" is a fine example of Sting's penchant for mixing high-art literary references with popular music sensibilities. The narrative of "Wrapped . . ." is based on emotions associated with an unbalanced relationship in which one character acknowledges his or her lack of power; thus, wrapped around your finger. As the tune progresses, the protagonist repeatedly discovers that he or she is always between a "rock or a hard place" or, as Sting puts it, between the "devil and the deep blue sea behind me." In the end, the protagonist promises that the servant will become the master, and you will eventually be "wrapped around my finger." During this complex narrative, Sting alludes to Christopher Marlowe's play, *Doctor Faustus*, and Goethe's poem, "The Sorcerer's Apprentice." These are clearly not typical subjects to use in pop music, and Sting needs the requisite musical space to tell his story, so the murky reggae texture is a perfect accompaniment. Once again, the space provided by the reggae texture offers room for Sting's lyricism, while also providing a contrast to the driving rock choruses. These contrasting textures support the tension and release that is essential to the tune. The tense rock choruses feature Sting's harmonized voice repeating the single phrase, "I'll be wrapped around your finger." Likewise, Summers's and Copeland's accompaniment repeats simple and straightforward musical phrases. But the verses are transparent, a bit foreboding, and contain Sting's sophisticated allusions. The accompaniment echoes these allusions as well with a thin analog veneer hovering over a coy drum pattern that references reggae but never fully embraces it.

Indeed, The Police never fully embraced any one style. Although they frequently signified elements of progressive rock, punk, and reggae in their music, they would rarely adopt any style wholesale. This tendency has continued to intrigue listeners and critics for decades.

2

THE POLICE AND THE STYLE MOSAIC

Certainly, the most prevalent styles that The Police utilized were progressive rock, punk, and reggae, but their repertoire features more than just these three music styles. The Police frequently combined multiple disparate styles in just one song, thus creating complex musical hybrids. In many instances, these hybrids feature large portions of some styles along with hints of others. Although each of these separate styles is discernable, the overall product of this integration is what constitutes the unique "sound" of The Police.

A style may be evoked by using even a small element of that style; such elements are frequently referred to as "topics." For instance, the reggae style may be evoked, along with all the social, historical, and music awareness that comes with it, by a simple one-drop drum pattern. The other characteristics of reggae, such as the rolling bass line, the socially conscious lyrics, the guitar skank, and the Jamaican vocal accent do not necessarily need to be present in order for the style to be evoked. The music of The Police and Sting often contains rich combinations of topics that signify multiple diverse styles, all within just one song. Methodologies from cultural studies, particularly the idea of the cultural mosaic, may help in understanding these subtleties. The concept of the cultural mosaic and the resultant "style mosaic" can help explain how The Police created their musical identity.

In 1938, the Canadian writer John Murray Gibbon promoted the idea of the cultural mosaic in his book, *Canadian Mosaic.* He believed the idea of a "melting pot" metaphorically distanced immigrants from their past by promoting full assimilation into a new culture. Gibbon's idea of a cultural mosaic represented a cultural process that simultaneously incorporated immigrants into a larger picture or mosaic while also enabling each "tile," or individual, to maintain their own identity. Professors Georgia T. Chao and Henry Moon describe how the idea of mosaic works:

> A *mosaic* is a composite picture made up of distinct colored tiles or miniature photographs. That is, both the overall picture and the multitude of colored tiles are simultaneously distinguishable. Viewing an individual's culture as a *cultural mosaic* allows for simultaneous observation of global individual culture and localized cultural influences. (Chao and Moon, 1129)

This same concept may be applied to musical style as well.

A style mosaic is composed of large and small style "tiles." In the case of The Police, the large tiles can connote the aforementioned progressive rock, punk, and reggae. The smaller tiles represent hints of another style. For instance, dub-inspired echo, guitar distortion, or an ethnic flute can evoke a larger global style without defining the tenor of an entire song. Of course, The Police rarely wrote songs that utilized only one style or "tile;" more often, their songs consisted of large style tiles, like an entire chorus of reggae, combined with smaller tiles, like a hint of jazz in Sting's voice. This style mosaic theory sheds light on how The Police seamlessly integrated small and large style tiles.

"ROXANNE"

The song "Roxanne" provides an excellent example of The Police style mosaic. Within the first few bars of "Roxanne" there is stylistic ambiguity. So much ambiguity, in fact, that the members of The Police themselves have divided opinions on the style of the introduction. Sting states in his autobiography, "While originally written as a jazz-tinged bossa nova, the song will evolve into a hybrid tango through the trial-and-error of the band process" (*Broken Music*, 295). Andy Summers concedes that "Roxanne" began as a bossa nova, but he goes on to state that in order to "give it an edge," they had to integrate a bit of reggae into the process. Summers writes:

> At the moment it's a bossa nova, which is a problem—not because it doesn't work that way but because in the prevailing climate it would be suicidal to go Brazilian, and we already have enough problems. So how should we play it? We have to heavy it up and give it an edge. We decide to try it with a reggae rhythm, at which point Stewart starts to play a sort of backward hi-hat and tells Sting where to put the bass hits. (*One Train Later*, 189)

Both men are correct; the introduction to "Roxanne" *simultaneously* evokes tango and reggae, but why did Summers state it would be suicidal to go Brazilian?

In regard to reggae, there were musical and social ties between reggae and the punk movement. Many punk musicians felt a kinship with marginalized West Indian populations and their struggle against the reigning upper classes. Furthermore, reggae artists like Peter Tosh and Bob Marley were becoming international superstars. Reggae was in the air, and groups like The Clash and The Police frequently integrated reggae into their punk oeuvre. In short, reggae was cool. On the other hand, Brazilian styles, like bossa nova, were not cool. Through the recordings of the jazz saxophonist Stan Getz and the Brazilian songwriter/pianist Antônio Carlos Jobim, bossa nova had reached its peak in the early 1960s. The bossa nova style was light, gentle, apolitical, and arguably the soundtrack of an older and upper-class generation. As jazz musicians, Sting and Summers certainly had a great deal of experience with and perhaps even an affinity towards bossa nova. In fact, Sting had recorded an early version of "Every Little Thing She Does Is Magic" in the autumn of 1976 in bossa nova style. Nevertheless, both Summers and Sting surely knew that if they wanted to be accepted into the London punk community of musicians, journalists, and listeners, they had to stay away from any stylistic hints of bossa nova. The result of this avoidance is this unique tango and reggae hybrid.

Clearly, the band believed that "Roxanne" should not begin in bossa nova style, but tango was an equally risky choice. Today, there are various styles of tango dances, but the original tango, with its distinctive accompanying music, was conceived in the late nineteenth century in the lower-class regions of Buenos Aires. Despite its lower-class origins, this elegant and virtuosic dance style gained international popularity, and by the late twentieth century most varieties of tango were generally regarded as an upper-class activity. The accompanying music to tango can be multifaceted and complex, but arguably its most identifiable aspect is its rhythm, and it is this rhythm that is used in the introduction and verses of "Roxanne."

The most basic tango rhythm features four beats to a bar with an accent immediately preceding beat 1: 1–2–3–4 (accent)–1–2–3–4 (accent), and so on. Many musicians call this kind of rhythm, "playing on the down beats," and many versions of tango standards like "El Choclo" and "La Cumparsita" feature this rhythm. Furthermore, jazz musicians like Tony Bennett ("Boulevard of Broken Dreams") also used this basic rhythm to signify tango within a jazz context. Considering the various musical backgrounds of Summers, Copeland, and Sting, it is likely that they were at least rudimentarily aware of tango. Indeed, one of Sting's earliest musical memories involves tango:

> I remember sitting at my mother's feet as she played the piano. She always played tangos for some reason. Perhaps it was the fashion at the time, I don't know. The piano was an upright with worn brass pedals. And when my mother played one of her tangos she seemed to become transported to another world. Her feet rocking rhythmically between the loud and soft pedals, her arms pumping to the odd rhythms of the tango, her eyes intent upon the sheet music in front of her. (Berklee College speech)

During the introduction to "Roxanne," these "odd rhythms" of the tango may be heard in Summers's playing as well as in Copeland's accenting on the hi hat.

Sting has routinely stated that the introduction and verses of "Roxanne" signify tango more than any other style, but listeners have routinely described it as reggae. Noted music journalist Hugh Fielder states, "It was unlike anything that people had heard before. Yes, there were elements of reggae in it. There were elements of punk in it and that staccato beat. It was just unusual and it stuck in the brain" (*Rock Milestones*). In 1979, Jeff Tamarkin echoed Fielder's observations: "'Roxanne,' their current single (and a cut from the forthcoming A&M album), is a reggae-ised number about a prostitute, which also recalls several familiar '60s pop passages along the way." If the introduction and verses of "Roxanne" are clearly conceived in tango style, why do so many listeners describe "Roxanne" as reggae?

The down beat/tango rhythm in "Roxanne" is not like typical reggae skank (1 *accent* 2 *accent* 3 *accent* 4 *accent*), which is known to most musicians as "playing the up beats." However, while Copeland indeed performs the typical tango accent at the end of beat 4, he also plays a far more prominent accent with the bass following beat 1 (1 (accent)–2–3–4, 1 (accent)–2–3–4, etc.). If The Police were interested in signifying only tango, they would have accented the end of beat 4 and little else; instead, they instinctively gravitated towards rhythmic ambiguity and away from typical tango. Sting comments on this rhythmic puzzle: "Rhythmic ambiguity is something I adore. I love being unsure about where one is, and then it's 'ah,' that's where it is" (McBride). Admittedly, performing an accent following beat 1 is neither typical of tango nor reggae, but the simplest explanation for this pattern is that it is essentially a tango accent delayed by one beat.

In short, the answer to the question of why listeners identify "Roxanne" as reggae is because it *sounds* like reggae. Timbre is a powerful identifier. In fact, many listeners can instantly identify musical styles by the timbre of the guitar, voice, or bass before a single lyric is sung. The timbral quality of the introduction and verses of "Roxanne" signify reggae above all else. For instance, during the introduction, although Summers is playing the tango down beats, the reverberated, percussive sound of his guitar recalls the reggae skank. Furthermore, Copeland's intricate hi-hat patterns certainly signify the drumming styles of reggae, and they would become the hallmark of his reggae-inspired drumming style. In addition, Sting does little to temper the fundamental sound of his electric bass. It is raw, dark, and creates a counter to the vocal melody, all of which are common characteristics of reggae bass. Lastly, all the instruments and vocals are immersed in heavy reverb, a common effect used in reggae recordings.

Not only did listeners hear reggae because of timbre, but they *expected* to hear reggae. "Roxanne" may be an iconic tune today, but it failed to chart when it was initially released in April 1978. In October of that same year, The Police began their first North American tour without a hit single and on a very limited budget. This first tour of the Northeast lasted only twenty-seven days and was lightly attended, but some of those present were curious industry professionals like DJs, promoters, station managers, and music critics. The Police would later credit these industry professionals for showing the interest in "Roxanne" that ultimately led to its re-release by popular demand in 1979. Sting recalled:

> A DJ in Texas happened to have our single on his desk by a complete fluke, a coincidence. He played it; he liked the record obviously and it got what's called "good phone" in America, where listeners phone in their responses to records . . . and it started to break out in San Francisco and Boston, so it happened like some kind of disease. (Gambaccini)

During this initial club tour, The Police performed reggae-inspired tunes like "So Lonely" and "Can't Stand Losing You," and they quickly developed a reputation in the industry for combining punk with reggae. By the time "Roxanne" was re-released, it too was assumed to be largely reggae, in spite of its larger tango "style tile."

This unusual combination of tango and perceived reggae is an exotic hybrid that perfectly frames the equally exotic lyrical content. During October 1977 funds were tight, and the band was staying at a dingy motel behind one of the Paris train stations, Gare St. Lazare. Sting was inspired to write "Roxanne" after observing the desperate lives of the Parisian prostitutes who were loitering outside. The narrative that Sting created features a male protagonist who implores Roxanne to give up her life of debauchery. The name "Roxanne" came from a faded *Cyrano de Bergerac* poster that was hanging in the motel lobby, and Sting poetically describes his fateful inspiration:

> I will stand for a few moments to take in its fading gaiety. It is a laughing portrait of a man with an enormous nose and a plumed hat. He is a tragic clown whose misfortune is his honor. . . . He is a man who loves but is not loved, and the woman he loves but cannot reach is called Roxanne. That night I will go to my room and write a song about a girl. I will call her Roxanne. I will conjure her unpaid from the street below the hotel and cloak her in the romance and the sadness of Rostand's play, and her creation will change my life. (*Broken Music*, 286)

The subject of prostitution is rarely addressed in popular music, but when it is, artists treat it in various ways. For instance, Blondie's "X Offender" is an ironically playful tune that focuses on the romantic attraction between a prostitute and her arresting officer. Elton John's

"Sweet Painted Lady" speaks of the inherent sadness of "getting paid for being laid." The Velvet Underground's "There She Goes Again" is a bleak portrait of a woman forced into prostitution by her own drug addiction and her abusive pimp; "She's out on the streets again . . . she won't take it from just any guy, what can you do . . . you better hit her." Although these examples are compelling studies of pop music narratives and prostitution, none of them combines the mystique of Parisian nightlife with the exotic styles of foreign music like "Roxanne."

The unnamed protagonist begs Roxanne to quit her life as a prostitute, imploring her to no longer "put on the red light." The idea of the "red light" is the primary imagery of "Roxanne" and is used in the first line of text, in the pre-chorus, and throughout the chorus. The red light references a long-standing European custom of advertising sexual services by simply having a red light bulb turned on in the front window of a sexually oriented establishment. This is why many areas catering to prostitution are called "red light districts." These districts have an undercurrent of seediness and mystery that are mostly experienced by desperate men and women, and, in fact, desperation is what "Roxanne" is all about. In the verses and pre-chorus, the protagonist desperately pleads with Roxanne that "those days are over" and she doesn't "have to wear that dress tonight." It appears, though, that the male character's desperation also creates an air of judgment when he remarks, "you don't care if it's wrong or if it's right." Indeed, this desperate state creates conflict within the male protagonist, and the conflict is equally represented in the tango-reggae hybrid framing the lyrics of the verses and pre-chorus. With the arrival of the chorus, the desperation reaches full bloom through the repeated lyric, "Roxanne (put on the red light)." The primary musical style shifts to punk rock, its aggressive and driving nature providing a potent counterbalance to the exotic and subtle nature of the verses and pre-choruses.

In "Roxanne," Sting combines the universal emotion of desperation with the pointed imagery of the red light district, all framed by the styles of tango, reggae, and punk, but there is one more "style tile" that is present: jazz and blues. The influence of these styles should not surprise a listener who is familiar with the individual biographies of The Police. Both Sting and Andy Summers worked as professional jazz musicians before their tenures with The Police, and both retained their interest in jazz after The Police disbanded. Keep in mind, however, that

The Police were very cognizant of their tenuous position within the punk and pop music communities. When Summers stated that "we already have enough problems," he was referring to the struggle The Police were having finding their niche in the world of popular music, and the blatant use of jazz would surely compound this problem; borrowing from jazz or blues had to be clandestine.

For instance, the last chord of the introduction to "Roxanne" is unlike any other chord played in that section; it is built on fourths instead of thirds. To clarify, in popular music most chords are constructed of stacked thirds. A third interval stacked on another third interval creates a tertian harmony, and this, by far, is the most common kind of harmony in nearly all types of popular music. The harmony that Summers plays at the end of the introduction is constructed as a quartal harmony. In other words, it is a chord built using an interval of a *fourth*. This type of harmonic construction is far less common in popular music, but it is very common in jazz because it conveys an "airy" or "open" sound, and it is also a bit more difficult to play on guitar. Of course, Summers was technically proficient, so it was easy for him to integrate a bit of jazz harmony within the introduction of this popular tune.

There are also tinges of jazz and blues in the way that Sting interprets the melody. While Sting does not fully signify jazz in "Roxanne," he does not sing the tune solely in a rock style either. For instance, the lyric "Roxanne" is sung with a descending fourth interval in the verses and pre-chorus, and sometimes Sting sings this descending interval in a sad, almost lamenting fashion, which is very familiar to those who listen to Billie Holiday, for instance. At other times in the final pre-chorus, he growls the word "Roxanne," mimicking a frequent technique used by blues singers. Sting's vocal subtleties were not lost on his bandmates. Many years later, Summers commented that Sting channeled his jazz background: "Sting is able to wail and vocalize over the ambience as if he is Miles Davis brooding his way through a solo" (*One Train Later*, 191).

A final comment in regards to the jazz and blues "style tile" relates to use of musical space. In jazz, one of the most important lessons that any improviser must learn is how to create a delicate balance between sound and silence. This is not as easy as it may appear. Many jazz musicians study for years in order to play lots of technically demanding passages, and in some respects, the number of notes he or she can perform at any given time determines their level of mastery. But more mature jazz performers realize that the space between notes or phrases can be as powerful as the notes themselves. On the other hand, most styles of popular music feature continuous sound, with very little silence. So much so, for example, that the recording style of the renowned music producer Phil Spector is known as the "wall of sound." Atypical of popular music, but very common in jazz, there are multiple pauses or moments of silence in "Roxanne:" between the introduction and verse one, between verse one and two, between verse two and the pre-chorus, between verse three and four, and between verse four and the pre-chorus. These moments give "Roxanne" an airy, mysterious ambiance that is uncommon in the world of popular music. Fittingly, this exotic ambiance is a perfect vehicle for the equally exotic lyrics. The style mosaic of "Roxanne" is fairly complex. In just over three minutes, The Police deftly combine dashes of tango, reggae, punk, jazz, and blues with exotic lyrics framing a desperate man's attempt to persuade a prostitute that she no longer has to "put on the red light." Still, "Roxanne" is a very early example of the many style mosaics that members of The Police will create throughout their careers, and later mosaics are significantly richer.

"MESSAGE IN A BOTTLE"

During a 1981 recording session for *Ghost in the Machine*, Sting asserted to Jools Holland that "Message in a Bottle" was his finest composition to date:

> When I wrote "Roxanne," I thought, "I like that. It's really good. Will I ever write one better?" Then I wrote "Message in a Bottle," which was better than "Roxanne.". . . My favorite song is probably "Message in a Bottle," because lyrically and musically it's the most unified piece I've written. (Holland)

Considering the musical complexity and commercial success of "Roxanne," Sting's statement was a bold one, but he may have realized that many of the concepts used in "Roxanne" were more fully realized in "Message in a Bottle." Certainly, the narrative of "Message in a Bottle" is more complete than that of "Roxanne," and its style mosaic is more subtle and complex as well.

"Message in a Bottle" was the most mature and sophisticated song that Sting had yet written. He states:

> I'd been carrying this guitar riff around in my head for a year . . . I was pleased that I'd managed a narrative song with a beginning, a middle, and some kind of philosophical resolution in the final verse. If I'd been a more sophisticated songwriter, I would have probably illuminated this change of mood by modulating the third verse into a different key. But it worked anyway. (*Lyrics by Sting*, 26)

Sting's maturity as a songwriter manifests itself within the chronological nature of "Message in a Bottle." The first verse begins with the image of a castaway enduring more "loneliness than any man could bear," leading to a message in a bottle in the chorus. During the second verse, Sting bluntly writes, "A year has passed since I wrote my note," once again hoping that someone gets his message. In the third verse, an early morning revelation leads the protagonist to discover that there are a "hundred billion bottles washed up on the shore," all written by a hundred billion lonely castaways. Sting is justifiably proud of the scope of this narrative; within a pop song framework that lasts a little under five minutes, our castaway has written a note, an entire year passes, and he then receives billions of responses. Within this broad narrative, Sting also includes pointed images that frame his thoughts on the nature of loneliness.

To many, the idea of sending a message in a bottle connotes an act of desperation, isolation, romance, or curiosity. In fact, the idea of sending a message in a bottle is what inspired Sting to write the song:

> "Message in a Bottle," that's an interesting title. I write from titles. I don't write from the first line of a song. It's a mistake because then you have to come up with the second one. If you write backwards from the chorus, which is usually the hook, then you usually come up with it. So I had the "Message in a Bottle." What's this message in a bottle about? It's usually about some guy in ragged trousers and a beard on a desert island. (Holland)

From the very beginning, Sting connects with the image of a neglected castaway trapped on a desert island. This is a perfect metaphor for addressing loneliness, which is really what "Message in a Bottle" is about. The castaway is isolated on a metaphorical desert island, from where he implores the listener to save him before he falls into despair. He places his pleas within a bottle but realizes that while "love can mend your life," it can also "break your heart." Ultimately, the castaway realizes that he is not alone and that there are a "hundred billion" other castaways who are equally lonely. Upon further consideration, though, this lone figure's desperation evolves from an individual experience to a broad statement on universal loneliness.

During the first verse, the castaway is an isolated figure, "another lonely day, with no one here but me," who then sends "an S.O.S. to the world." The castaway's feelings are personal and self-reflective, but by the end of the tune his emotions become public; there are now a hundred billion bottles washed up on the shore. His emotions are no longer relegated to a desert island; they are now part of a broader and shared existence. The castaway has evolved from a shy and tortured individual to being part of a universal emotional experience. This may be part of what Sting calls the "philosophical resolution" summed up with the statement, "seems I'm not alone at being alone." The exotic imagery and the philosophical resonance of the lyrics are not typical for pop songs, and the style mosaic that frames these images is equally atypical.

The style mosaic of "Message in a Bottle" begins with a guitar arpeggio, meaning the performer plays the notes of a chord as a melodic sequence rather than simultaneously. Although this introduction is very indicative of something Summers would have created, Sting actually wrote it; "I had this sequence going on with the chords. By arpeggiating, you get the riff . . . I get home from the bus, turn 'Dennis' the drum box on . . . I set the tape recorder and put this riff down" (Holland). This introduction offers no hints as to the variety of musical styles that will follow. In fact, only Copeland's slippery drum fills differentiate the introduction from similar mainstream rock tunes of the era, like Blue Öyster Cult's "Don't Fear the Reaper," or Boston's "Peace of Mind." Nevertheless, Summers's expertise shines through even in this context. Although the arpeggiated pattern may sound simple, it features wide intervallic leaps that are difficult for most guitarists to perform. Summers also accomplished the formidable task of recording the same arpeggiation at two different intervallic levels, creating a thicker and more aggressive sound.

The mainstream rock style continues into the first verse, but Copeland's drumming provides a hidden style tile. Nearly any other drummer of the era would have interpreted the driving guitar arpeggiation and awkward bass line as an opportunity to lay down a heavy and irrefutable drum beat. Instead, Copeland offers a reggae-inspired one-drop drum pattern that is propelled by his lithe hi-hat work. As discussed in the first chapter, instead of on the up beats, the one-drop pattern features an accent on beat 3. Since there is no accent on beat 1, the beat is dropped, thus the term "one drop." The beat 3 accent is usually made by the bass drum, with a snare hit, or cross stick. With the aid of overdubbing, Copeland also incorporated slight accents on beats 2 and 4. In summary, Copeland has combined a typical mainstream rock beat with the reggae one-drop pattern, though most listeners barely notice such intricacies.

The chorus begins in a more mainstream rock style, but under scrutiny, another style tile is covertly inserted by Andy Summers. In terms of harmony, most post-1950s popular songs are supported by triadic harmony. Popular artists from Elvis Presley to Taylor Swift use triadic harmony as the backbone of their repertoire. A triad is made up of a root, third, and fifth. Arguably, the most important part of a triad, at least to pop musicians, is the third because it determines whether the chord is major or minor. Since a major triad has a much different sound than a minor one, the third of a triad actually defines the nature of the chord. As mentioned in the "Roxanne" discussion, many jazz musicians avoid triadic harmony, preferring instead to base their harmonic vocabulary on fourths, not thirds, largely because triads sound too "poppy" or "square," and triads are simply not part of the jazz tradition. Musicians like Summers and Sting, who are comfortable in the use of non-triadic harmony, have the musical skills to move away from triadic harmony. During the chorus of "Message in a Bottle," Summers refuses to play any thirds whatsoever, explaining, "One of the things we did in that band was to try to play a lot of harmony without the third, the triadic element" (Summers interview). Although the chorus certainly sounds like mainstream rock, Summers's choice creates a harmonic expansiveness that is rare in pop music.

Beyond Summers's and Copeland's covert stylings, "Message in a Bottle" is fairly mainstream, but the pretense of conformity ends during the post-chorus. After the rock-inspired chorus, the post-chorus instantly shifts to a dub-inspired slow groove, during which Sting's vocals and Summers's guitar lines take a back seat to the bass and drum groove. This is the typical musical environment of dub, which originated in Jamaica in the late 1960s after DJs discovered that crowds enjoyed stripped-down versions of reggae songs. However, artists like King Tubby and Lee "Scratch" Perry did more than simply strip away a vocal track; they inserted snippets of other instruments and vocals and, most importantly, added lots of reverb and delay effects to the existing parts. Ultimately, dub versions featured prominent drums and bass surrounded by a heavy echo. By the early 1980s, dub artists like Mikey Dread and Jah Shaka used the ubiquitous dub reverb on songs like The Clash's "Bankrobber" and UB40's "Strange Fruit" and "25%." During the post-chorus of "Message in a Bottle," The Police hint at the dub tradition by eliminating the churning rock guitar accompaniment, the harmonized vocals, and the keyboard of the chorus, leaving only the drums, bass, and reverberating guitar fills. This exotic texture is not only a nod to the dub tradition, but it also provides an emotional middle ground between the high-energy chorus and the self-reflective verses.

Disco is the final element of style mosaic of "Message in a Bottle," which may appear to be an odd choice of style for The Police. By the late 1970s, disco's enormous popularity had created an equally large critical backlash, culminating in the infamous "disco demolition night" at Comiskey Park in July 1979. Moreover, The Police associated with a punk community that may have despised disco more than any other musical style. Nevertheless, Stewart Copeland coyly integrates a disco-like hi-hat pattern within the final verse. The omnipresent hi-hat beat was one of the most prevalent rhythmic characteristics of many disco recordings, like "Disco Inferno" and "Night Fever," and Copeland, who was surely well versed in this clichéd drum pattern, slyly incorporates it into the final verse. As with "Roxanne," The Police demonstrate with "Message in a Bottle" that they can integrate nearly any style at any moment.

"BRING ON THE NIGHT"

Although "Bring on the Night" was recorded by The Police in 1979 for *Reggatta de Blanc,* much of the tune's lyrics and harmonic structure were written by Sting in the mid 1970s for the band Last Exit. This earlier rendition is titled "Carrion Prince," and it shares the first two lines of the first and second verses with the later version, "Bring on the Night." The verses of "Carrion Prince" also share their harmonic progression with those of "Bring on the Night." The similarities end there, though, and "Bring on the Night" is otherwise a significantly different tune than "Carrion Prince." Andy Summers notes that The Police routinely transformed Sting's songs into something richer and more interesting: "'Message in a Bottle' and 'Bring on the Night' are gems. We have a process of getting to know the song and then rearranging it to give it The Police sound, which means moving it into a place where the sound is tight, lean, and spare, the meat close to the bone" (*One Train Later*, 208).

In other words, The Police took the dated sound of "Carrion Prince" and created a rich and compelling style mosaic.

This style mosaic begins in the introduction, which consists of Sting's flanged bass and Copeland's intricate hi-hat patterns. Copeland uses this particular pattern when he wants to signify reggae or dub, and predictably, when his bass drum enters during the second half of the introduction, it is immersed in the thick reverberation that is typical of dub. After the dub-inspired introduction, the verse begins with Sting's soaring vocals and an abrupt change of accompaniment by Summers. Summers explains, "I spent about five years playing classical guitar. I don't remember much of it, but I did put in a lot of time doing that. It's come up in some numbers we're playing together. 'Bring on the Night' is played with sort of a classical arpeggio . . . that relates to some classical pieces from Villa-Lobos" (Holland).

Indeed, immediately following the dub introduction, Summers accompanies the verses that follow with this classically influenced guitar pattern. Heitor Villa-Lobos is arguably the best-known composer of classical guitar music, and much of his music is based on agile, fingered arpeggios similar to those heard in "Bring on the Night." In fact, every time the verse reappears, these arpeggios are included. Then as the chorus begins, ska is introduced as yet another style tile.

Ska became a popular symbol of Jamaica's independence and national identity in the early 1960s. A typical ska band was made up of a singer, guitar, drums, bass, and a horn section, and many of these ska bands adapted a fast-paced "up beat" to American R&B tunes. Ska performers like Derrick Morgan, Desmond Dekker, and The Skatalites reached the peak of their popularity by the mid-1960s, but then fell off when the slower rock-steady style came into vogue.

By the late 1970s, elements of ska reappeared as part of an offshoot of punk, called "two tone." "Two tone was ska at 78 rpm, sung with a nasal English accent, and many of the groups spiced things up with a distinctly British sense of humor which derived from the old music halls and which blended in neatly with the ska tradition of boasting, self-mockery, and bad mouthing developed in Jamaica by men like [Prince] Buster and Duke Reid" (Hebdige, 111).

Two tone performers such as The Specials, The Beat, The Selecter, and Madness typically combined the up-tempo groove of ska with so-cially conscious lyrics, lots of guitar, and a punk sensibility. Of course, The Police were part of the punk movement and surely were familiar with this two tone offshoot; in fact, Sting frequently wore a "The Beat" T-shirt during live performances. Furthermore, The Police obviously had an interest in Caribbean styles and were aware of the original ska style as well, so it's no surprise that the chorus is constructed of precise-ly the elements that make up ska: a bright tempo, a prominent up beat, and a very Jamaican-sounding rolling bass line. Even Sting's voice has a hint of a Caribbean accent.

Following another verse and chorus, two more style tiles are intro-duced before and during the guitar solo. First, there is an odd interlude after the second statement of the chorus. This interlude features the return of the heavy reverb effect on Copeland's bass drum and a screaming, almost feedback effect from Summers's guitar. The reverb and shrieking guitar are indicative, once again, of the avant-garde na-ture of dub; the vocals and pleasing guitar arpeggios have been left behind, and what is left is a raw and nearly atonal musical statement provided by the guitar and drums. This kind of musical experimentation is unusual in a popular tune, but The Police made it work. After the interlude, Summers begins his solo over the harmonies of the verse and introduces another style tile: psychedelic rock. Summers's tenure with groups like Dantalian's Chariot and Soft Machine clearly introduced him to radical and avant-garde approaches to soloing, and he demon-strates these traits in this solo. It is howling and loud, and it features a touch of the blues more typical of guitarists like Jimi Hendrix. Of course, Summers never entirely dismisses the musical environment of

"Bring on the Night;" he just adds an angularity and aggressiveness that isn't heard much in the 1980s.

In the end, this simple song, which lasts only four minutes, is a colorful mosaic of musical styles like dub, classical guitar, ska, and even psychedelic rock. These disparate styles are gathered from distant cultures and backgrounds, and yet, The Police combined them all into a coherent and entertaining pop tune.

3

STING AND THE ALBUM MOSAIC

On July 23, 1983, The Police began a massive world tour to promote *Synchronicity*. This tour, which lasted until spring of 1984, was a spectacle of innovative cross-promotions, sold-out arenas, and exotic locations. The Police were arguably the biggest band in the world. "Every Breath You Take" had become a worldwide hit, *Synchronicity* was regarded as one of the year's biggest albums (alongside *Thriller* and the soundtrack to *Flashdance*), and the band's videos were on heavy rotation on the fledgling cable channel, MTV. Sting, Andy Summers, and Stewart Copeland were having remarkable success as individual artists as well. By the summer of 1983, Sting had finished filming his first major motion picture, *Dune*. Andy Summers had completed his critically acclaimed album with Robert Fripp, *I Advance Masked*, and Stewart Copeland had finished his soundtrack to Francis Ford Coppola's *Rumble Fish*. On the surface, the future looked bright, but internally, The Police were falling apart.

Although it is impossible to pinpoint the exact moment when the band broke up, the performance at Shea Stadium is a good place to start. The Beatles, Grand Funk Railroad, Jethro Tull, The Who, and Simon and Garfunkel were the only acts that had ever headlined at Shea, so on August 18, 1983, when The Police performed at the legendary venue, the performance was a watershed moment for them. The band had reached the pinnacle of rock stardom. Sting recalls, "I sat with Andy and Stewart and I said, 'This is as good as it gets. We're playing Shea Stadium, this is where The Beatles played. We're the biggest band in the world this year. After this, it's going to be diminishing returns. I think we should stop now, at the top'" (*Sting: Behind the Music*). Remarkably, Sting, who was the creative force behind nearly all of the band's hits and was certainly the "face" of The Police, stepped away from the biggest band in the world at the peak of their popularity. Andy Summers had predicted this decision: "After a few years and unparalleled success together, the fragile democracy has become a dictatorship, and Sting's agenda—his natural proclivity to do it alone—has begun to manifest itself with a kind of grumpiness around the band" (*One Train Later*, 336). Indeed, Sting did want to "do it alone," and the forced democracy of The Police was too much for him to endure. Although Sting was the most public figure of The Police, Copeland was the founder, and Sting was forced to work within the confines of the band. Sting admits, "Stewart's energy was the prime mover of The Police. He started the whole thing. . . . He got us together. His drumming style was, and still is, unique. It was his idea to make a record on our own, pay for ourselves very cheaply, and to distribute and market it ourselves" (*Sting: MTV Rockumentary*). By this point, Sting clearly had musical and career aspirations that did not include his bandmates, and he no longer had the patience to work within the pseudo-democratic constructs of The Police, so he decided to become a solo act. Sting talks about his decision:

> I saw my own future very clearly outside of the band, because I wanted more freedom. I couldn't have played with two better musicians than Stewart and Andy, but I wanted to make music that wasn't tied to the limitations of a three piece band, where I didn't have to compromise my own standards as a songwriter to maintain what was in truth only the semblance of democracy within the band. (*Broken Music*, 323)

Sting did not create the same kinds of style mosaics as a solo artist as he did with The Police. This is not to say that he was no longer interested in style appropriation; on the contrary, Sting was more interested than ever in musical styles, but many of his songs do not individually demonstrate the song-based style mosaics of The Police. Instead, Sting creates album-based style mosaics that are equally compelling. Instead of individual songs, which feature a rich mosaic of integrated styles, Sting creates albums, which are a collection of songs written in various styles. The idea of the style mosaic has shifted from the song to the album.

Sting's new approach to musical style demanded a high level of musical virtuosity and versatility, and he looked for the finest musicians available. In early 1985, with the help of journalist Vic Garbarini, Sting compiled a band of four jazz instrumentalists and two background vocalists: Omar Hakim (drums), Darryl Jones (bass), Kenny Kirkland (keyboards), Branford Marsalis (saxophone), Dollette McDonald (vocals), and Janice Pendarvis (vocals). Sting's new band wasn't simply a collection of unknown session musicians; they were well known in the jazz community. Omar Hakim had performed with Carly Simon and was a member of the renowned jazz-fusion group, Weather Report. Darryl Jones was the bassist for Miles Davis and had recorded two albums with the legendary jazz trumpeter. Kenny Kirkland toured and recorded with Wynton Marsalis and Branford Marsalis, who himself had already recorded his first solo album and was a member of Art Blakey's Jazz Messengers before his tenure with Sting. Sting had clearly recruited some of the finest jazz musicians of their generation.

The jazz pedigrees of Sting's new band indicate that he was leaning towards a different style of music than that of The Police: "As good as The Police were, and as versatile, it was still a three-piece rock group. I wanted the ability to write in whatever style I wanted and bring in musicians who could fit that bill of fare" (*Sting: Behind the Music*). Sting undoubtedly had a strong affinity for jazz and even used certain jazz elements in his work with The Police, but he would not label himself a jazz musician. Jazz is a style that demands high levels of instrumental and vocal virtuosity; it has a canon of great artists, a specialized repertoire, and it can be very esoteric. Most importantly, jazz is not popular. Its inherent improvisatory and abstract nature deters most listeners, and Sting surely knew this.

This period was arguably the most important of Sting's career. Many assert that Sting's international fame as the leader of the most popular band in the world and as an actor virtually assured success; moreover, Sting was surrounded by performers who reached the highest peaks of success after they left their former bands. Lionel Ritchie, Peter Gabriel, Don Henley, and Phil Collins had experienced unmatched solo success around the time that Sting left The Police. Coincidently, Hugh Padgham, the producer of Collins's best-selling album, *Face Value*, also produced *Ghost in the Machine* and *Synchronicity*. Therefore, Sting had a firsthand view of what a solo career could provide. On the other hand, there were examples of failed solo efforts as well. In early 1985, David Lee Roth, the charismatic lead singer of Van Halen, released his critically maligned solo EP, *Crazy from the Heat*, but never achieved the same popularity as he had with his bandmates. Mick Jagger released his first solo album in 1985, but *She's the Boss* was not the critical or commercial success that was normally associated with Jagger's band, the Rolling Stones. Commercial or critical failure was a real possibility, and Sting's decision to hire a band comprised of jazz musicians did little to quiet the skeptics. Music journalist Anthony DeCurtis wrote, "If there is a shortcoming in Sting's current fascination with jazz, it may be that in seeking more sophisticated musicianship and trying to avoid pop banalities, he has undersold the virtues of melody and concision that characterized his best writing with the Police" (23).

What some critics failed to recognize was that Sting's choice of band was not necessarily intended to eschew pop banalities or to avoid memorable melodies; instead, Sting was looking for creativity and versatility. Although Sting was searching for more musical autonomy than he could have gotten while with The Police, he still needed creative energy and innovation from this new band. Sting explains,

> I recruited jazz musicians from New York; not that I wanted to play jazz and not that I wanted them to play my kind of rock music. I was hoping by taking them out of their environment and putting me outside my own comfortable environment, we would end up with something that was different from both rock or jazz, something without a label. (*Sting: MTV Rockumentary*)

Marsalis, Kirkland, and the others were experienced musicians who spent their careers working in the spontaneous and creative world of jazz; thus, they did not need a "road map" to lead them to their artistic destination. One of the most intriguing characteristics of jazz performers is their ability to create complex musical performances based on limited musical material. In other words, jazz musicians can do a lot with very little.

Although Sting was an extraordinarily creative writer and arranger, it was beneficial to have such resourceful musicians to help "fill in the gaps" while recording and performing his new repertoire. Sting was redefining his musical style, both privately and publically, and he needed muses who could offer new sources of creativity and inspiration. However, inspiration alone is sometimes not enough, and developing a new musical style requires musical versatility and experience as well. Sting's new band was remarkably versatile. For instance, Hakim performed with Carly Simon and Dire Straits, Kirkland recorded with Chico Freeman and Carla Bley, and Jones performed with Herbie Hancock's Headhunters, then later with The Rolling Stones. These musicians were able to master almost any musical style, and Sting clearly benefitted from their creativity and versatility. Sting's new musical style was wide ranging, and it took a highly talented group of performers to work within this new musical framework.

Sting's personal and professional life certainly contributed to his new approach to creating solo albums. In March 1984, the final world tour of The Police was complete, and Sting's obligations to his former band had ended. The tour had been extraordinarily successful and had helped position Sting as one of the most famous musicians in the world. Of course, he participated in all the trappings afforded an international superstar, including a final divorce from his first wife, Frances Tomelty. Sting had married Tomelty in 1976, and she was an important part of his life from the impoverished early years through the superstar years of the early 1980s. The divorce was a significant event in his personal life, and as such it contributed to his new musical style. Sting also attempted a career as an actor, and in 1984, his film career was in full swing with the release of David Lynch's big-budget science fiction epic, *Dune*. By 1985, Sting had also finished filming his next movie, *The Bride*, with costar Jennifer Beals. After The Police tour of 1984, Sting participated in a few musical projects as well. He produced the single "I Don't Believe a Word" for the little-known group A Bigger Splash, and in November, he participated in Bob Geldof's "Do They Know It's Christmas?", a remarkable attempt at bringing relief to famine-stricken Ethiopia. Within one year, Sting had ended his tenure with The Police, recently endured a painful divorce, had seriously begun a film career, launched a life-long interest in charity campaigns, and assembled an exciting new band. All of these events contributed to a distancing from the manic style experiments of The Police to a more mature, but no less compelling, treatment of style in his solo works. Moreover, Sting's new treatment of style framed a significant shift in lyrical content. The various subjects of Sting's solo albums are an extension of his intellectual curiosity, as well as his concern with political and environmental matters, divorce, and romantic longing.

The songs of The Police were youthful experiments, using unpredictable style combinations, but Sting was no longer interested in experiments; he was interested in creating mature and polished products. Sting's album mosaics were comprised of song sets that demonstrate an extraordinary variety and depth of styles and subjects. Although all of Sting's albums demonstrate this variety of styles and subjects, the albums . . . *Nothing Like the Sun* and *Mercury Falling* are particularly rich in style appropriation and lyrical content.

. . . NOTHING LIKE THE SUN

Sting's first solo effort, *The Dream of the Blue Turtles* (1985), was a commercial success. In the United States, the singles "If You Love Somebody Set Them Free," "Fortress around Your Heart," and "Love is the Seventh Wave" were unqualified hits that helped Sting earn four Grammy nominations for Album of the Year, Best Male Pop Vocal Performance, Best Engineered Record, and Best Jazz Instrumental Performance. It is the last category, though, that reveals how some listeners categorized Sting's debut album. Although Sting certainly touched on disparate musical styles like gospel, reggae, and blues, many listeners labeled the album "jazz" because of the obvious jazz influences on many of the tracks. Songs like "Shadows in the Rain," "Consider Me Gone," "The Dream of the Blue Turtles," and "Moon over Bourbon Street" were entirely composed in a jazz style, and others like "Children's Crusade" and "Fortress around Your Heart" featured specific jazz elements, such as a soprano saxophone solo. While *The Dream of the Blue Turtles* undeniably contains more jazz influences than any other style, in . . . *Nothing Like the Sun* (1987), his second album, Sting uses a more diverse style palette.

. . . *Nothing Like the Sun* is a stunning example of stylistic diversity, which frames highly literate subject matter. To begin with, the album title references Shakespeare's Sonnet 130, which begins with the line, "My mistress' eyes are nothing like the sun." Shakespeare's work is a parody of the traditional love sonnet popularized by Petrarch. In it,

Shakespeare pokes fun at the conventional tendency to compare women to snow or roses, and he plainly states that his mistress does not have snow-white breasts, rosy cheeks, or perfumed breath. Shakespeare believes his love is so special that he will not lower himself to describe it in such a hackneyed manner. Like Shakespeare, Sting is concerned with various views of femininity. His preoccupation with femininity may also be tied to his mother's death in 1987 from cancer; this momentous event surely influenced . . . Nothing Like the Sun as well.

The introduction of the opening track, "The Lazarus Heart," provides a hint of what is to come later in the album. The tune begins with a combination of automated and restless keyboard patterns coupled with harp sounds, agogô (go-go bells), African-influenced bottle sounds, and Andy Summers's swirling guitar. When Branford Marsalis's soprano saxophone enters with an eight-bar melody, it is lightly mixed with an ethnic flute sound. The groove is clearly influenced by African-derived styles, which had become popular by the mid-1980s. Peter Gabriel (So), Talking Heads (Remain in Light), Paul Simon (Graceland), and Sting's former bandmate, Stewart Copeland (The Rhythmatist) had appropriated African musical styles. However, the African influence of "The Lazarus Heart" does not last long; when the markedly processed drums of Manu Katché enter, much of this ethnic rhythmic complexity is swept away by a predominant R&B/radio-friendly groove. This is an understandable decision by Sting. The first track on any album, especially one that has as many commercial expectations as a Sting release does, is a sonic "welcome mat" to the rest of the production. If the opening tune is too esoteric, many listeners would not feel welcome and may not venture further into the record, or even worse, may not purchase it. In terms of esotericism, though, the subject matter of "The Lazarus Heart" is more unusual than most popular songs.

Sting dedicated . . . Nothing Like the Sun to his recently deceased mother, and the lyrical content appropriately addresses universal issues of womanhood and femininity. As in the case of "The Lazarus Heart," Sting sometimes frames this sophisticated subject matter within equally complex musical styles, but these styles do not shift and overlap within individual songs as in his work with The Police. Instead, Sting more commonly introduces an initial style at the beginning of the tune, and that style, or elements of that style, continue throughout. This approach to style usage creates more mature and coherent compositions—a colorful album mosaic—and directs attention to the lyrics. The subject matter of "The Lazarus Heart" was inspired by a dream of Sting's: "'Lazarus Heart' was a vivid nightmare that I wrote down and then fashioned into a song" (liner notes, . . . *Nothing Like the Sun*). In his dream, and later in the song, the protagonist discovers a gruesome chest wound from which a flower grows. He later discovers that his mother has given him this injury but has also given him the gift of the flower. Sting's imagery describes the painful struggle of maturation and change, something that he had recently experienced a lot of, and the inevitable rebirth of something new, symbolized by the flower. The chorus continues with the idea of rebirth, "every day another miracle," but now frames it in terms of childbirth and connection, "only death will tear us apart." As the song progresses, this idea of death becomes more prominent, culminating with the thought that only family and love can shield someone from the pain of death. Admittedly, these complex lyrics are not common fodder for pop songs, but Sting combines them with an upbeat and fun musical style that serves to soften the blow.

"Englishman in New York" is one of Sting's most likeable and re-quested songs, and he frequently performs it today. The sunny Carib-bean groove and puckish lyrics surely contribute to the tune's longevity. The inspiration for the song was actor, author, and raconteur Quentin Crisp, who Sting met while filming *The Bride* in 1985. Crisp had moved into an apartment in New York's Bowery neighborhood and found him-self within the foreign world of cosmopolitan America. The first verses and chorus playfully outline the alienation that an Englishman could experience while living in New York: "I don't drink coffee I take tea my dear." Later, however, the lyrical material becomes a bit more substan-tial; "it takes a man to suffer ignorance and smile" may certainly be targeting the ignorance that many have towards the homosexual com-munity. On the other hand, Sting may be addressing what it means to be a "man." The sense of maturation illustrated in "The Lazarus Heart" returns in "Englishman in New York." In this instance, Sting denounces the need for combat gear or guns as a way to define what a "real man" is, and he begs that maturity not be measured by weapons but by manners, poise, and being oneself "no matter what they say."

Once again, Sting cloaks the serious subject matter with a light and joyous musical style. "Englishman in New York" is largely performed in Sting's most archetypal style, reggae. The introduction begins with the traditional reggae up beat, along with light strings performed on keyboard by Kirkland, and Marsalis's soprano saxophone fills. The tempo is lively, and Sting's bass line propels the introduction forward nicely. Although reggae certainly works in this instance, it is an unusual style choice for Sting to make. After all, neither Englishmen nor New York have much to do with reggae or the Caribbean. The best explanation for this stylistic decision is that the bulk of the recording was done at the sun-drenched AIR Studios in Montserrat, or perhaps Sting was simply looking for the lithe feeling that reggae provides.

Throughout "Englishman," Sting incorporates non-reggae musical styles as well. Strings and a harpsichord sound are heard throughout the bridge, then the following section moves into a double-time swing feel, which is interrupted by the abrupt appearance of a funk/rock beat. Keep in mind that this style interplay is not like the sophisticated, multilayered style mosaics of The Police era; rather, these styles are somewhat crudely placed one after another with no interlocking connections. Why would Sting create such a simplistic parade of styles when he is obviously capable of so much more? For one thing, Sting is attempting to represent the diversity of musical styles that are available in New York. In other words, as Crisp strolls down the avenue, he is hearing reggae, classical, jazz, and rock music. Also, Sting's band is bursting with competence and creativity. They can play in any style, at any time. In fact, Sting has added Mino Cinelu (percussionist), Manu Katché, and Andy Newmark (drums) to the *Blue Turtles* band. He has also included a long list of renowned guests such as Hiram Bullock, Mark Knopfler, and Eric Clapton on guitar, as well as Gil Evans (arranging) and Kenwood Dennard (drums). With such high-caliber musicians, Sting could afford to show off their flexibility.

Sting returns to his feminine-based themes with "They Dance Alone (*Cueca Sola*)." "They Dance Alone" addresses Chilean dictator Augusto Pinochet and the somber demonstrations performed by Chilean females who lost loved ones to his oppressive regime. Augusto Pinochet took control of Chile in 1973, and he governed the nation with fear and intimidation until 1990. Some estimates report that nearly 2,000 opponents to Pinochet were "disappeared." By the mid-1980s, Sting had become involved with Amnesty International. This organization, formed in the early 1960s, campaigned to defend freedom of expression, abolish the death penalty, demand justice for crimes against hu-

manity, and protect women's rights, and, of course, it publically demonstrated against Pinochet. These campaigns were clearly in line with
Sting's own philosophies, and he admirably dedicated countless charity
performances and tours to Amnesty, even convincing his bandmates
from The Police to perform on the final three performances of the
Conspiracy of Hope Tour in 1986. It is through Amnesty International
and subsequent tours that Sting learned the details about the protests
against Pinochet's regime:

> On the Amnesty Tour of 1986 the musicians were introduced to
> former political prisoners, victims of torture and imprisonment with-
> out trial, from all over the world. These meetings had a strong affect
> [sic] on all of us. It's one thing to read about torture but to speak to a
> victim brings you a step closer to the reality that is so frighteningly
> pervasive. (liner notes, . . . *Nothing Like the Sun*)

It is worth noting that Sting noticed the tension within Chile as early as
1982 when The Police performed there.

In opposition to Pinochet's regime, Chilean women (*arpilleristas*)
publically danced the Chilean national dance, the *cueca*, with photos of
their missing loved ones pinned to their clothing. Ironically, the *cueca* is
not a somber dance; it customarily features a man wearing a Chilean
cowboy hat, flannel poncho, and spurs, and a woman dressed in a traditional Chilean flowered dress. The participants elegantly circle each
other while waving kerchiefs, all joined by a generally up-tempo, triple-
metered musical accompaniment. This representational dance is usually performed during joyous occasions related to Chilean independence.
The *arpilleristas* cleverly co-opted this symbol of national pride and
transformed it into a proclamation of national embarrassment and con-
demnation. This non-aggressive/female protest left a particularly deep
impression on Sting.

Unlike the *arpilleristas'* approach to *cueca*, Sting does not take a
clever or ironic approach to "They Dance Alone." The tune begins with
a somber mood of sustained string sounds, cymbal splashes, and a bit of
soprano saxophone. Sting further defines this mournful tone with a
militaristic snare drum pattern that is easily associated with Pinochet's
military-style governance and his position as commander-in-chief of the
Chilean army. A pan flute (performed on keyboard), widely associated
with various folk musics of South America and particularly the Andes,

also appears in the introduction and will reappear throughout the tune. As the song progresses, the lyrics take prominence over the somber accompaniment. At first glance, the lyrics appear to simply be a series of statements on Pinochet's atrocities, but upon closer scrutiny, there is a narrative of discovery that may reflect Sting's own gradual understanding of the story. In the beginning, Sting asks, "Why are these women here, dancing on their own?" He discovers that the women are dancing with their missing sons, husbands, and fathers. In the second verse, Sting further describes this method of protest as the only form of protest they're allowed for fear of being "another woman on the torture table." During the third verse, Sting predicts the fall of Pinochet's regime, concluding with the macabre question, "Can you think of your own mother dancing with her invisible son?" At this point, the unbearably solemn subject matter and musical style is interrupted by a galloping samba groove that concludes the tune. Once again, Sting uses style to make a philosophical point. At this instant, the past, framed by death and torture, is traded for a bright future of equality and joy.

The Latin-tinged "Fragile" is one of Sting's most requested and beloved songs. One reason for its longevity is that the meaning of "Fragile" is adaptable to the context of any given time or event. Sting originally wrote "Fragile" as a dedication to Ben Linder, who was a volunteer engineer brutally murdered by Contras in northern Nicaragua while working on a hydroelectric project for the impoverished inhabitants of the area. In the dedication, Sting lamented that the lines between good and evil were sadly becoming blurred: "In the current climate it's becoming increasingly difficult to distinguish 'Democratic Freedom Fighters' from drug dealing apolitical gangsters or Peace Corps workers from Marxist revolutionaries" (liner notes, . . . *Nothing Like the Sun*). Sting comments that his trips to South America have been inspirational:

> I have to say that the memories stayed with me, and every time I've gone there I've met extraordinary people and witnessed extraordinary events and went to amazing places like the Amazon. So events like that stay with you as a songwriter . . . it's a real hotbed of human activity, so for someone like me it can only be inspiring. (*Sting: MTV Rockumentary*)

By the mid-1990s, Sting confessed that he now related "Fragile" to the political and humanitarian situation in Bosnia. Then in 2001, while recording a live album at his Villa Il Palagio on September 11, Sting was informed of the terrorist acts in New York City. He decided to perform "Fragile" on a live webcast and then continue with the rest of the concert offline. At the beginning of the broadcast the following dedication was shown: "We are performing the song 'Fragile' as a prayer and a mark of respect for those people who have died or are suffering as a result of this morning's tragedy. We are shutting down the webcast following this song" (*All This Time*). In the compact disc version of the concert, "Fragile" is first in the song order and only the lyrics to "Fragile" are included in the liner notes. "Fragile" has also been used as a call for environmental awareness in programs like *The Living Sea*. Why has this song become such a universal call for compassion and understanding?

First, Sting composed "Fragile" in the style of bossa nova and samba, capturing the sensitivity of bossa nova with the slow tempo and traditional guitar pattern while creating an underlying two-beat feel in the bass which resembles samba. Both of these musical styles originated in Brazil and are regarded as light, fun, danceable, and generally apolitical. The hybrid bossa/samba style is accentuated in the introduction with Sting's acoustic guitar pattern. His guitar pattern is light, gentle, and recalls Brazilian folk music. The melody of "Fragile" is also remarkably simple and repetitive. Furthermore, the simple binary form enables listeners to easily understand the lyrics and emphasizes its folk character.

Second, the lyrics to "Fragile" describe a universal sensitivity to life and a disdain for violence. The first verse examines the anguish of war, which will always be washed away, but sadly, "something in our minds will always stay." The second verse contends that no solutions will be found with violence, and in the end, we cannot forget how fragile we are. Considering the philosophical significance of "Fragile," the lyrics are remarkably concise, with only two verses and one repeated chorus. This economy of music and words surely contributes to the timelessness of "Fragile."

After the weighty subject matter of the two preceding tracks, "We'll Be Together" is a welcomed release. It was the first single released from . . . *Nothing Like the Sun*, and for good reason. This tune is about romance and, as the title states, being together. The R&B/funk style of "We'll Be Together" is more in line with what listeners expect from

Sting. It is fun, groovy, and memorable. Sting continues this lightness in the next tune, "Straight to My Heart," but with a twist.

The lyrical content of "Straight to My Heart" is also about romance, but this time the relationship has not fully formed. Although the lyrics are charming, the music is far more compelling. "Straight to My Heart" begins with a percussion introduction that hints at a South American style like samba, but that style is played in the odd meter of 7/4. With very few exceptions, most popular music is written in duple meter, but Sting's musical expertise and virtuosic band enabled him to write music that is deceptively different. The rhythmic and lyrical phrasing of "Straight to My Heart" hides the unusual meter to such an extent that listeners may not even notice. As the tune progresses, the inclusion of handclaps and flute sounds accentuate the samba-like characteristics, but they never reveal its hidden rhythmic secrets.

Both "Rock Steady" and "Sister Moon" share a similar musical style, jazz. Considering Sting's deep interest in jazz and his band's expertise, it is no surprise that this style is featured in . . . *Nothing Like the Sun*. In the case of "Rock Steady," Sting fuses a contemporary telling of Noah's ark (with added commentary from televised preachers) with a jazz shuffle, bluesy piano fills, horn lines, and a gospel organ. "Sister Moon," possibly the sequel to "Moon over Bourbon Street" from *The Dream of the Blue Turtles*, incorporates even more jazz elements. Sting's bass anchors the 12/8 feel as it slowly creeps along. Marsalis's soprano saxophone fills are heard throughout, and Kirkland's strings create a lush jazz harmonic underpinning. More than any other characteristic, the extended harmonic vocabulary of "Sister Moon" is a hallmark of jazz writing. Sting may have been particularly interested in jazz harmony because he was working with Gil Evans, one of the finest jazz artists of his generation.

Evans, a composer, bandleader, and arranger, confirmed his legendary status with his work with Miles Davis, who Sting had briefly worked with during the recording of Davis's *You're Under Arrest* album. Sting had been a fan of Evans's work for years and describes their first meeting: "I met Gil Evans one night in Ronnie Scott's club in London. He'd been a hero of mine since I was fifteen. . . . I went backstage after the show to introduce myself and was amazed and flattered that he had ever heard of me. He told me he liked the bassline of 'Walking on the Moon.' I went home on cloud nine" (liner notes, . . .

Nothing Like the Sun). During a subsequent performance with Evans, Sting sang "Little Wing," and Evans noted that he already had a concept for the song. In fact, Evans had recorded "Little Wing" in 1974. Evans's version on . . . *Nothing Like the Sun* combines lush keyboard strings with the aggressive timbre of Hiram Bullock's guitar and, of course, Sting's soaring vocals.

The final track on . . . *Nothing Like the Sun* is "Secret Marriage." Along with the two prior tracks, this tune is clearly about relationships with women. In this case, Sting is plainly communicating his belief that a marriage is not about veils, flowers, maidens, or dowries; a marriage is something that is continually revived through mutual love and respect. Sting admits that he adapted the melody from a song by Hanns Eisler and Bertolt Brecht, titled "To the Little Radio." Sting's adaptation is a freely played ballad that includes only piano and bass. This sweet ode to his own relationship is an uncommon way to conclude a pop album, but considering the lyrical depth featured in . . . *Nothing Like The Sun*, it is duly appropriate.

As a whole, . . . *Nothing Like the Sun* is a stunning example of the album mosaic. Sting incorporates styles from samba to jazz, and he uses these styles to accentuate the philosophically weighty matters of religion, relationships, politics, and violence. Although the album is certainly a masterwork, Sting will continue to refine these ideas in *Mercury Falling*.

MERCURY FALLING

Nearly ten years after the release of . . . *Nothing Like the Sun*, Sting debuted one of his most acclaimed albums, *Mercury Falling*. In the intervening years, Sting had been occupied with more albums, charity work, and his acting career. He had released *The Soul Cages*, which demonstrated his versatility and intellect but did not sell as well as prior albums. Then in 1993, Sting had returned to creating pop hits with the best-selling *Ten Summoner's Tales*. He had moved away from overtly public pleas for the environment but remained personally active in charity concerts. Sting had also continued pursuing his maligned acting career with films like *Stormy Monday* (1988), *The Adventures of Baron Munchausen* (1988), and *Gentlemen Don't Eat Poets* (1995). Sting was certainly a busy man, but during a break from his tours, movies, and charity obligations, he found time to record yet another album. He began working on *Mercury Falling* at his estate, called Lake House, during the production phase of *Ten Summoner's Tales*. The comfortable and familiar surroundings made this a perfect location for writing. When the time came to record *Mercury Falling*, Lake House was a logical choice, and the domestic environment contributed to many of Sting's stylistic and lyrical choices: "I was enjoying these long periods at home with the family. I'd spent so much of my life in hotel rooms and concert halls. I felt that at last I was living a real life. The kids would come home from school in the afternoon and we'd all have dinner together like a normal family" (*Lyrics by Sting*, 192).

The album mosaic of . . . *Nothing Like the Sun* featured Sting's mature interest in styles like reggae and samba. The mosaic of *Mercury Falling* is more representative of styles that Sting experienced earlier in life and closer to home. Sting was forty-three years old during the recording of *Mercury Falling*, and his growing maturity led him to explore his past through the musical styles of his youth. This is not to say that Sting did not touch on more exotic styles in *Mercury Falling*—this is a vital aspect of his art—but this album mosaic is mostly guided by Sting's enthusiasm for his early influences like soul, country, and English folk music styles. Furthermore, an overarching narrative of emotional transformation and growth accompanies this catalog of style.

The idea of personal growth and aging is apparent even in the title, *Mercury Falling*. Of course, winter is historically associated with aging, so the idea of the temperature falling concurrently with maturity is obvious. Mercury is also synonymous with speed, and Sting may have believed he was slowing down as well: "I suppose the album title suggests, among other things, that my mercurial life was beginning to find some balance, like I'd finally put down roots. I'd always believed that 'settling down' was anathema to creativity, but I wanted to give it a shot" (*Lyrics by Sting*, 192). Mercury is also the god of thieves, and Sting frequently stated, "I'm a thief. I'm a musical thief, I'll steal from here, I'll steal from there, and hopefully make something new. I'm interested in the music of the margins, not pure jazz, not pure rock and roll, not pure anything. I like impure music because that excites me" (McMullen). Much like Sting's music, Mercury has multiple meanings; it can be a planet, god, liquid, poison, or an element.

In keeping with the winter inferences, *Mercury Falling* begins with "The Hounds of Winter," which speaks to the bleakness of a dead lover and the accompanying cold sadness. The lyrics detail a man who is enduring the death of his spouse and proclaims, "Where she's gone, I will surely, surely follow." During his mourning, this character also endures the discomfort of winter. The musical style associated with this bleak portrait is a slow and sparse R&B groove, grounded by Kirkland's organ and Dominic Miller's guitar.

The tune that follows, "I Hung My Head," is a surprising stylistic departure for Sting. He had an interest in country and western music since he was a child, and frequently cites the music of *Gunsmoke* and *Rawhide* as meaningful musical experiences. Both of these American television programs premiered in the 1950s and proved to be popular with children around the world. His interest in this style is previously heard in "Love Is Stronger than Justice" from *Ten Summoner's Tales*. In fact, both tunes share an extended narrative, a country aesthetic, and an odd meter of 9/8. Sting had displayed an interest in odd meters since the mid-1980s, but it is rare for this to be used in a country song. Much of country music is danceable, and odd meters make that difficult. Sting deftly hides the irregularity of the meter with a repeated guitar pattern that is typical of the style, and the expert drumming of Vinnie Colaiuta, a widely acknowledged master of odd meters, sounds so effortless that listeners may not notice the unusual meter that lurks beneath. Sting's odd meter choice may have been programmatic, mimicking the loping stride of a horse; Sting was known to ride horses around Lake House— "The guitar riff just occurred to me that way and reminded me of the gait of a galloping horse dragging a corpse" (*Lyrics by Sting*, 195).

The narrative of "I Hung My Head" outlines a tragic accident. A young man borrows his brother's rifle and decides to practice his aim by targeting a horseman in the distance. The rifle fires, killing the rider. The young man is brought to court and proclaims, "I wish I was dead." Although remorseful, the man is convicted and sent to the gallows. This is certainly an extended narrative for a four-minute song, but it is suspenseful enough that listener interest is easily sustained. Sting also integrates a puckish humor into the morbid tale. Country music has a history of humorous songs, and Sting taps into this history with a bit of funny wordplay. The song begins with the phrase, "early one morning, with time to kill." This serves to ease the listener into the gruesome tale.

Secondly, the beginning refrain, "I Hung My Head" signifies a remorseful bowing of the head, but by the end of the tune, the young man's head is literally "hanging."

"Let Your Soul Be Your Pilot" harkens to Sting's youth and his fascination with American soul artists like Aretha Franklin, Booker T. & the MG's, Otis Redding, and James Brown. In fact, the East London Gospel Choir and the Memphis Horns are used throughout the track, inspired by the gospel-tinged music pioneered by these iconic artists. Sting's inspiration for the tune, though, came from his relationship with a friend who was hospitalized with the AIDS virus. Sting gave *The Tibetan Book of Living and Dying*, by Sogyal Rinpoche, to his ailing friend. The book and the tragic situation were inspirations for "Let Your Soul Be Your Pilot." The lyrics capture the hopelessness that can follow an ailment that no medicine chest can make well, and also capture the demoralization of too much useless information. As the tune progresses, the soul and gospel elements become more pronounced, and although the situation is dire, a sliver of hope is offered with the repetitions of "Let your soul guide you along the way."

The next tune, "I Was Brought to My Senses," exemplifies Sting's use of disparate styles. In this song, Sting shifts from a Celtic folk ballad to an odd metered, Brazilian-inspired groove. There could not be two more different musical styles. And, of course, the narrative corresponds with this style shift as well. The spirit of "I Was Brought to My Senses" resides in the transformative process of falling in love. The narrative of the folk ballad section describes a man who is in love and is confounded by how that love will flourish. He is soon inspired by nature, "where the two birds were flying." Following this inspiration, the Brazilian groove begins with a verse featuring a quote from "Message in a Bottle": "I walked out this morning." Not only is this a clever self-reference, but it identifies the new section with the optimism of a new day. In this uplifting section, our romantic hero sees his love in every signpost in nature: leaves, rivers, and trees. In the end, the transformative character of the lyrics is played out in the music. While the initial indecision of the man is framed by the somewhat staid confines of the Celtic ballad, when he finds confirmation of his love, the equally joyful sounds of Brazilian music accompany the discovery.

Sting returns to his earlier musical influences with "You Still Touch Me" and "All Four Seasons." Both of these tunes echo the Motown and

Stax recordings of the 1960s, and both are directed at his family. "You Still Touch Me" begins with a guitar lick reminiscent of Sam and Dave's "Soul Man," and from that point on, the tune epitomizes the soul sound that Sting idolized as a young man. Unlike most of the songs on the album, "You Still Touch Me" is a straightforward song about a man, presumably Sting, who remains in love with his partner after many years together. "All Four Seasons," with lots of horns and organ, follows the soul template as well. In this case, Sting addresses the fickle temperament of his young daughter, Coco.

Sting returns to the country style with "I'm So Happy I Can't Stop Crying." As with "I Was Brought to My Senses," "I'm So Happy" features a transformative narrative, but this time, it is about a man who is moving beyond a divorce but with the resultant loss of the custody of his children. In the previous country-styled "I Hung My Head," Sting was a bit coy about his use of the country style, but in this case the pedal steel guitar, a strong country two-beat rhythm, and a typical country harmonic progression make "I'm So Happy" unquestionably a country tune. In fact, Sting is proud of his stylistic versatility. He frequently mentions that Toby Keith's remake of "I'm So Happy" reached number two on the country charts in 1997.

The tune begins seven weeks after a man's wife left him for another man. He is clearly in despair; when his former spouse asks about his emotional condition, he simply says, "I'm so happy that I can't stop crying." This refrain returns throughout the song. As time progresses, the wounded man gets joint custody and legal separation, and after looking up at the stars, he decides that he'll do "the best within the given time." By the end of the tune, the protagonist has moved from despair to hope. Sting uses clever key changes and innovative formal procedures to musically frame this transformation. According to Sting, it is a remarkably positive song: "I haven't left this character stuck or trapped in his obsessions like the character in 'Every Breath You Take.' He's moved on. For that reason, it's a very positive song" (*Sting: VH1 Storytellers*).

The album mosaic of *Mercury Falling* becomes even richer with "La Belle Dame Sans Regrets." In this case, Sting and Dominic Miller emulate the stylings of Brazilian musical legends João Gilberto, Antônio Carlos Jobim, and Luis Bonfá. This elegant tune begins with a light samba rhythm supporting a timeless melody and an elegant piano solo by Kenny Kirkland. The poetic lyrics are in French, and they portray a fickle, mysterious, and untrustworthy woman with no regrets. The French woman may be a metaphor for the French government, whose above-ground nuclear testing in the mid-1990s reportedly dismayed Sting. The words are a bastardized version of French, and Sting has had a tenuous relationship with this language on record. He used a faux French dialect on The Police recording, "Hungry for You," and was asked to speak the language by Miles Davis on the track, "One Phone Call/Street Scenes" in 1984. In all instances, Sting has used a considerable amount of poetic license with the French language.

Since growing up in the shipbuilding city of Wallsend, Sting's fascination with the sea has been an important part of his music, culminating with his Broadway show, *The Last Ship*. "Valparaiso," originally written for the film, *White Squall*, is the result of Sting's fascination with distant sea ports: "Valparaiso was one of the names that captured my imagination. I imagined that it meant valley of paradise and pictured old sailing ships berthed in its peaceful harbor, resting after the terrors of Cape Horn" (*Lyrics by Sting*, 210). Sting's imagination may be accurate; Valparaíso is indeed an important seaport for sailors traveling around Cape Horn. The majority of "Valparaiso" is written in the style of a triple-metered English folk song, featuring Kathryn Tickell on Northumbrian pipes. This is a perfect style choice, as it frames the harshness of sea travel, while adding a sense of mystery and history to the narrative.

Mercury Falling concludes with the uplifting "Lithium Sunset." Sting states that he heard that sunsets provide a free antidepressant: "A South American shaman told me that the human eye can't filter yellow light, so the lithium in direct sunlight goes straight to the brain. . . . He explained further that this was why it was good to watch the sun go down, to feel calm and at peace before nightfall and before the mercury falls again" (*Lyrics by Sting*, 212). So "Lithium Sunset" is about the joy of seeing the sun set; "heal my soul O lithium sunset." Sting outlines this lighthearted narrative with another country style, but this time, it is reminiscent of the country styles of the 1970s, played by bands like the Eagles. This style choice is the perfect conclusion, because it ends the album, which has covered so many philosophical topics, on a hopeful note.

In the past, Sting had resisted the idea of a concept album, and for good reason. According to most measures, Sting's solo albums are a random collection of styles and narratives. Even *The Soul Cages*, arguably Sting's only concept album, contains so many disparate ideas and styles that it is difficult to hear any obvious overarching themes. What may unify many of Sting's albums, though, is that very randomness and unpredictability. Each of Sting's solo albums offers a sonic tour around various worlds of style, and if you don't like one style, another will be around soon enough.

4

SELLING THE POLICE AND STING TO THE WORLD

Recordings are the primary connection between a band and its audience. They enable listeners to re-experience the music in multiple venues like a car, supermarket, or bedroom. Over time, listeners may experience music in thousands of different contexts, but the recording will always remain the same. The albums of The Police and Sting are no exception, and undoubtedly, their recordings are the primary and unchangeable mode of communication between themselves and their listeners. But there is a more complex relationship at play than this simple recording-listener binary. In actuality, the albums are only one part of a complex web connecting The Police and Sting to their audience. Other parts of this web include tours, music videos, marketing and merchandising, and promotional videos. These important elements, along with the recordings, forged an ingenuous and enduring relationship with listeners from around the world.

The Police and Sting participated in innovative marketing and merchandising strategies that contributed to changes in the music industry as a whole. Most of these strategies were the product of the tireless, and sometimes ruthless, work of Miles and Ian Copeland. Stewart, Miles, and Ian are members of the remarkable Copeland family. Their father, Miles Copeland, Jr., played and arranged for the Glenn Miller Orchestra in the mid-1930s, but at the start of World War II, he volunteered for the Corps of Intelligence Police, an English counterintelligence program. After the war, he joined the fledgling Central Intelligence

Agency, and he remained remarkably active in the intelligence world. While stationed in Damascus, Syria, Copeland was involved in the nation's first military coup in 1949. He then became a close advisor to Egyptian president Gamal Abdul Nassar, and helped create the Mukhabarat (General Intelligence Directorate). Beginning in 1957, Copeland, along with his family, lived in Beirut, Lebanon, acting as a Western advisor. In fact, all of the Copeland children's formative years were spent in Beirut. Miles Copeland, Jr.'s extraordinary career was capped with the publication of three books and a considerable number of articles on global affairs. He was clearly a fearless, bold, and intelligent man who lived an exceptional life. These characteristics carried over to his family, ultimately affecting the careers of Andy Summers and Sting.

Miles Copeland III was born in 1944 while his father was stationed in London. The elder Copeland's exploits provided his son a view of the world that few children experience, and Miles's childhood was certainly unusual. He developed a knack for language and also a firsthand understanding of non-Western cultures, which would prove useful in managing The Police. Copeland's primary education was at the American Community School in Beirut. From 1962 to 1966, he returned to the birthplace of his father, Birmingham, Alabama, and graduated from Birmingham Southern College with a BA in history and political science. In 1969, he graduated from the American University of Beirut with an MA in economics. As Copeland finished his academic education, he also began his lessons in the practical world of music management.

By 1968, Copeland had already promoted his first concert at the American University of Beirut. This early success attracted the attention of a local promoter who needed help preparing for a show featuring Rupert's People, a London pop group. Copeland recalls, "The kids had never been to anything like it, and they went totally berserk. It was the biggest hoo-ha the university had ever had. That was my conversion" (Morris, 24). After this initial exposure to music management and promotion, Copeland moved to London and became the manager of Rupert's People. Although the band only released three singles and garnered little commercial success, Copeland was attracted to the energy and potential of the London music scene. Even at this early stage, the Copeland family worked as a team. In 1970, Stewart played drums for a later version of Rupert's People called Stonefeather, and Ian drove the group to performances. Miles Copeland had also become the manager of the progressive rock group, Wishbone Ash. Wishbone Ash, which formed in 1969, had released a series of influential albums in the early 1970s: *Wishbone Ash* (1970), *Pilgrimage* (1971), and *Argus* (1972). Under Copeland's maturing management style, Wishbone Ash achieved remarkable popularity. Riding this initial success, Copeland's artist roster grew to include Al Stewart, Joan Armatrading, Renaissance, Curved Air, and Climax Blues Band.

By 1974, Copeland's aggressive management style had paid off. He was already looking toward an international approach to the music industry when he created British Talent Managers (BTM), a management agency and record label. Through BTM, Copeland consolidated every aspect of the industry, from managing the artists to manufacturing records. Unfortunately, Copeland may have moved too fast. In 1975, he invested a considerable amount of capital in creating a massive touring rock festival called Startruckin' 75, a mobile music festival designed to move from one European venue to another, for which he compiled a list of artists including Wishbone Ash, Mahavishnu Orchestra, Caravan, Renaissance, and Lou Reed. Startruckin' 75 was the result of agreements between the various branches of BTM as well as European promoters and the large record companies RCA, MCA, and EMI. The complex legal arrangements enabled Copeland to organize a series of performances in over twelve European countries, which involved transporting over one hundred fifty musicians and crew, as well as tons of equipment. Copeland saw lots of promise in this new venture: "By linking up already existing festivals in Finland, Bilzen, and France, for instance, and adding on top our own dates we are making it the biggest festival tour ever put into Europe" ("Top U.S., U.K. Talent," 70). The cost of such a massive undertaking could only be overcome by equally massive public interest, but many of these acts were beyond their prime. Furthermore, Lou Reed's addiction to a myriad of drugs made him utterly undependable, and he never performed with the tour, forcing Copeland to substitute Ike and Tina Turner for Reed. Even with the Turners on board, promoters backed out of deals and left Copeland with large bills. Startruckin' 75 was an unqualified failure, and it eventually led to Copeland's bankruptcy and the dissolution of BTM in 1976. Copeland lamented his failure: "I spread myself thin. I never built an organization that could cover itself against a down period. We got to the point where we could not meet expenses, and the groups were greedy" (Morris, 25). It appeared that Copeland's meteoric rise had come to an abrupt end.

In some ways, Copeland was fortunate to have experienced such a definitive break with the progressive rock groups of the 1970s. His bankruptcy prohibited him from returning to a music scene that was burdened with enormous traveling costs, bloated egos, and a diminishing listener base. Consequently, he was forced to search for a less expensive and more radical kind of music from the London underground.

The new punk movement was perfect for Miles Copeland. Punk was a fledgling genre from which the performers, managers, promoters, and club owners did not expect a great deal of monetary gain. Moreover, many of the recordings and promotions of punk were low-budget, do-it-yourself endeavors. Copeland had tried an extravagant economic model, and now it was time to run a leaner type of business. He created start-up record labels like Illegal Records, Step Forward, and Deptford Fun City. These labels were small enough to react to market trends, and if they failed, there would be minimal loss. Copeland immersed himself in this new punk world by renting office space in Dryden Chambers, also the home base of Malcolm McLaren's Glitterbest management agency. Many punk groups, like the Sex Pistols, spent time at Dryden, as well as at The Ship, a nearby pub. Copeland even shared his office with Mark Perry, the founder of the punk fanzine, *Sniffin' Glue*. Perry was clearly in the middle of the London punk scene of the late seventies, and Copeland took advantage of this relationship by forming the punk-oriented record label, Step Forward Records, with Perry. During this period Copeland did a little bit of everything. He organized concerts and tours, managed The Cortinas, and helped promote bands like Johnny Thunders and the Heartbreakers, Generation X, Television, and Cherry Vanilla. In February 1977, Copeland arranged for American punk personality Cherry Vanilla to relocate to London. During her tenure in London, her backing band consisted of, among others, Stewart Copeland and Sting.

In January 1977, Sting arrived in London and, being a bit desperate, called Stewart Copeland, a drummer who had shown some interest in him after viewing a performance of Last Exit in Newcastle. Copeland was living in an affluent home in Mayfair, London, with his brother, Ian, and Sonja Kristina, the lead singer of his former band, Curved Air.

Normally, they could never have afforded such upper-class accommodations, but their father, Miles Copeland, Jr., had asked them to make life uncomfortable for a squatter who had taken up residence there. By mid-January, Sting, Stewart, and guitarist Henry Padovani were already rehearsing regularly. Stewart wasted no time promoting his new band. They had their first photo session with photographer Lawrence Impey on January 21, and by February, they had recorded their first two singles, "Fall Out" and "Nothing Achieving." Up to this point, Miles Copeland had shown minimal interest in his brother's new band. He agreed to release their new single under his Illegal Records label, and arranged for them to be the opening and backing band for Cherry Vanilla, but Stewart borrowed the money for the recording from a friend of Padovani's and did all the design and promotion for the single himself.

By August, Andy Summers had replaced Henry Padovani, and in January 1978, The Police were recording their first LP, *Outlandos d'Amour*. According to legend, during a break in recording, Miles Copeland listened to "Roxanne" for the first time. He immediately knew that it was special: "When I heard 'Roxanne,' I knew that . . . was something different. So literally, it all came from that moment when I listened to that song and realized what it was. None of them did. I mean, nobody in the band thought that the song was a game changer at all" (Brooks). Indeed, Copeland was so confident that he immediately approached A&M Records.

It was common in the industry to ask record companies for upfront money when a new band was signed. This money could be used for promotion, touring, or simply to placate the artists. The downside of the arrangement was that many record companies offered lower future royalties based on this initial unsecured loan. Copeland was not interested in such an arrangement: "I said, 'No advance, no upfront money, nothing—just give me the highest royalty you can possibly pay and let's go do it'" (Morris, 25). Copeland had a few factors on his side. First, he was managing the new wave group, Squeeze. With his help, Squeeze had signed with A&M, and their single, "Take Me I'm Yours," was climbing up the charts in early 1978. This success gave Copeland a little negotiating room with A&M. Second, the recording industry was enduring a recession, and record companies were looking for ways to take fewer economic chances. A lower royalty deal, with no upfront money, appeared to be the perfect solution for a hungry manager and a cautious

record company. Of course, as The Police became international superstars, they ultimately benefitted more from this deal than did the record
company.

Even with the promotional support of A&M, when "Roxanne" was
released in April of 1978, it did not chart. A subsequent single, "Can't
Stand Losing You," did not garner much attention either, so in October,
Miles Copeland made a bold decision—The Police were going to
America. Customarily, English bands toured the United States by supporting a larger act or promoting a successful single or album. The
Police did not have a hot new product. Their singles had already been
released and were largely ignored. Their second album, *Reggatta de
Blanc*, was not due for release for over a year. Furthermore, A&M
made it very clear that they had no intention of providing any financial
backing for the tour. Fortunately, Ian Copeland was in a perfect position to help.

Ian Copeland was born in the Rif Dimashq Governorate, which is
located outside of Damascus. As was the case with his siblings, Ian's
childhood was uncommon: "while kids back in the States were playing
cowboys and Indians, we were playing Crusader and Saracens, in real
Crusader castles" (Copeland, *Wild Thing*, 37). Unlike his siblings,
though, Ian had little interest in academics, and after some contentious
teenage years, he joined the U.S. Army in 1967. Therefore, while Miles
was promoting his first show in Beirut, Ian was serving in Vietnam.
Following Vietnam, he did a stint as the tour manager for Wishbone
Ash, after which he joined John Sherry Enterprises as a booking agent.
In just four years, he was promoted to partner in the new Sherry Copeland Artists company. Following the sale of SCA, he lived in London,
where he saw the first rehearsals of The Police, and in 1977 he moved
to Macon, Georgia, to join another management group, Paragon Agency. While working at Paragon, he was asked to break English artists into
the American market. After the disaster of the Sex Pistols in America,
and the subsequent reluctance of promoters to become involved with
unreliable bands, it was difficult to book English acts. Terms like "new
wave" were coined to differentiate these newer acts from the unreliable
punks, but these English groups remained associated with the rawness
and amateurism of punk and not with the more refined sounds and
professionalism of the upcoming new wave bands. However, Ian was
able to convince American promoters that new wave was the next big

thing, and he organized a tour in May of 1978 for Squeeze. As Ian states, there were major obstacles to touring with Squeeze:

> A club circuit did not exist at the time, although many of the major markets had "showcase" clubs that put on national acts. Bands were expected to break in by getting on a major tour supporting another headline act, and the showcase clubs were used mainly for promotion by the record companies. . . . Squeeze was unlikely to get on a tour with any of the major acts of the day, and it would have been too expensive anyway, so a club tour was the only choice we had. (Copeland, *Wild Thing*, 234)

Through dogged determination, Copeland arranged a successful club tour for Squeeze that proved be the template for The Police's tour later in the year. In fact, the strategies used for Squeeze set the stage for The Police:

> Although the Squeeze tour was a relatively modest success in the eyes of the music industry, I saw it as a major breakthrough. Squeeze pleased enough of the people at Paragon, and elsewhere around the country, to set the stage for me to bring in The Police, and after them, a whole wave of new bands from England. (Copeland, *Wild Thing*, 236)

In October 1978, The Police began their first U.S. tour. It was an exhausting and underfunded trek through the northeast, involving twenty-three shows in twenty-five days. Its purpose was to spur interest in *Outlandos* and "Roxanne" and to highlight what the band did best, play live shows. They stayed in low-budget motels, performed poorly attended club dates, traveled in a van for long hours, and had only one roadie, Kim Turner (the brother of Wishbone Ash guitarist Martin Turner). The austere economics of the tour could only have been possible with a three-piece band that was hungry to find success. Ian Copeland discussed the economics behind the tour:

> The Police were a three-piece, lean and mean, and ready to conquer the world. Miles and I figured that if anyone could turn America on to new music, The Police could, and if we cracked the American market, more bands would have a chance to do the same. . . . In the bigger picture, it was a way of saving the music business from the

stagnation that had set in, a way to revive the excitement that once
defined rock and roll. (Copeland, *Wild Thing*, 241)

Indeed, the style of music that The Police performed was central to
the promotion of the tour. Miles Copeland invited industry professionals to every show in an attempt to persuade them that The Police's
hybridic style of new wave music was the next big thing. Miles also
wanted to prove to the music industry that living within a budget could
be done, contrary to the outrageous recording and touring budgets of
bands like Fleetwood Mac, Led Zeppelin, the Eagles, Van Halen, and
Kiss.

The tour was successful in a variety of ways. First, A&M Records
recognized that The Police could be financially viable. Ian Copeland
stated, "By the time The Police completed the tour, ending with another two nights at CBGB's, Jerry Moss at A&M had already decided to
pick up his option on the band" (Copeland, *Wild Thing*, 244). This
established a relationship between A&M and The Police that would last
throughout their tenure as a band. Second, Miles Copeland's strategy to
involve industry professionals like DJs paid off. Because of interest
generated by the DJs at these shows, "Roxanne" began to get more
airplay in the United States, and by February 1979, the song had entered the *Billboard* charts, eventually peaking at number 32. In April,
spurred by its popularity in the United States, A&M re-released "Roxanne" in England, where it reached number 12 on the UK singles chart.

The Police proved to Miles that they were ready and willing to go
anywhere and do anything to become the biggest band in the world.
Consequently, Miles proved to The Police that he was eager to take
chances, and that those gambles could pay off. Miles Copeland's economic mantra of operating within one's means influenced the industry
throughout the 1980s, and Ian Copeland's tireless promotion of new
wave helped usher in an entire generation of new wave bands. When
the Paragon Agency folded, Copeland created his own agency, named
Frontier Booking International (FBI), in 1979. He used the same aggressive marketing and touring tactics to promote some of the biggest
bands of the 1980s, like R.E.M., The Cure, Simple Minds, The B-52s,
and The Go-Go's. Ian Copeland summarizes the lasting effect of his
innovative touring strategies: "The club circuit created by FBI still ex-

ists as an alternative way to break in new bands without massive amounts of financial backing" (Copeland, *Wild Thing*, 323).

THE POLICE: AROUND THE WORLD

Following their initial U.S. tour in October 1978, The Police returned to England, and A&M promptly released *Outlandos d'Amour* in November. The unrelenting touring and promotion of The Police had begun. Between recording sessions for *Reggatta de Blanc*, the band returned to the United States in March and again in late April of 1979. By August, a world tour had been organized to promote *Reggatta*. Amazingly, with relatively few breaks, The Police would be on tour for the majority of 1980 through 1983. They had proven that they were determined to do anything to reach the highest levels of commercial success, and Miles Copeland was equally eager to take advantage of various forms of media to spur the group to the greatest heights of stardom.

Although The Police certainly exploited traditional promotional strategies, like magazine, radio, and television interviews; posters; and record store appearances, Miles believed that the band could also be served by more innovative marketing products. One such product was the promotional video, *The Police: Around the World*. The video was filmed at various locations between February 1980 and January 1981. A husband and wife directing duo, Derek and Kate Burbidge, who had already directed nearly all the music videos for The Police, were hired by Copeland to film the band in exotic locales like Mumbai, Cairo, Athens, Buenos Aires, and Osaka. The filming was part of an effort by Copeland to turn the tour into a media event. He also arranged for BBC broadcaster Anne Nightingale to accompany the band and film her own BBC documentary, *Police in the East*. At various stops, Copeland invited journalists like Paul Morley to accompany the tour and interview the band. Roughly one hour and fifteen minutes long, *The Police: Around the World* portrays The Police in an almost Beatlesque manner, as a fun loving but contemplative group of young men on a musical adventure. Interspersed with clips from live performances appear lots of zany antics and mugging for the camera as the band is filmed playfully contemplating a Japanese rock garden, sumo wrestling, posing in front of Egyptian pyramids, and pretending to be Argentine gauchos.

The Police: Around the World was an important element of the initial success of The Police, and it showed that the band and Copeland were equally fearless. To begin with, Western-pop concerts were rarely performed in places like India, Egypt, and Buenos Aires, and for good reason. There were formidable logistical barriers to performing large-scale concerts in these countries, ranging from politically charged labor issues to inadequate equipment. And, in fact, The Police lost money in most of these venues. Miles Copland states, "We didn't go to India to make money . . . or Egypt to make money. There's no money to make there. Egypt's not a market. Neither is India. They're piracy markets. Why would we open up a market for pirates?" (Campion, 118). If there was no money in these markets, why did they bother to go there? Above all else, *Around the World* attached an indelible image of sophistication, exoticism, and intellectualism to The Police. Miles Copeland believed this sort of image was essential to the success of the band:

> The product was there. But there were other bands that had good product. Why did The Police succeed where other groups didn't? Their commitment to success. I would say to them, "Let's go play in India." They'd go, "Let's try it." All of a sudden, you've got Sting riding a camel with the pyramids in the background. What a photograph! It gave them an intellectual credibility. (Tannenbaum, "Miles Copeland," 32)

Admittedly, most rock bands do not strive for intellectual credibility, but Copeland believed that portraying The Police as sophisticated and internationally beloved could make them attractive to listeners everywhere. This image of The Police is encapsulated in the first few minutes of the film, which begins with a graphic, superimposing the faces of each member over a globe. The grandiose implications of the graphic are clear. After the opening credits, Andy Summers contemplates a Japanese rock garden with a guide who summarizes the Buddhist philosophy of simplicity. This placid moment is shattered by Miles Copeland's screaming introduction at a live performance, "It's time for the number one band of 1980! It's time for The Police!" The following rousing performance of "Next to You" is set against images of the band interacting with their fans in the subways of Japan and capped with scenes of the countryside. In these first few minutes of the film, viewers are shown that this is not a typical rock band, but one with a certain intellectual gravitas; they are remarkably well spoken, and, most importantly, they appear to be "worldly." The sophisticated and exotic images portrayed by *Around the World* were a perfect fit for the music The Police were creating. Their style mosaics, consisting of unusual collections of exotic styles like reggae, ska, and tango, were products from distant cultures, and the image of The Police as international travelers certainly reinforced their equally multicultural music.

During this period, Miles Copeland had another somewhat successful venture into film, *Urgh! A Music War*, again directed by Derek Burbidge. The film featured live performances from new wave performers like XTC, Jools Holland, Oingo Boingo, Pere Ubu, and Devo. Copeland wisely bookends the performances with his most popular group, The Police, whose performances include "Driven to Tears" and a memorable version of "Roxanne," filmed in Fréjus, France. The film "toured" independent theaters, playing for a few nights in each venue before moving on to the next. It was an innovative idea, but the film has no narrative, not even a voiceover narration, and it suffers from a lack of cohesion. In addition, the performers and their musical styles are simply too diverse to maintain viewer interest. Nevertheless, *Urgh!* is a rare and invaluable look into the early eighties new wave generation, and it stands as another example of Miles Copeland's innovative marketing strategies.

THE POLICE AND MTV

With *The Police: Around the World*, Miles Copeland was a step ahead of the video revolution of the 1980s. *Around the World* was filmed nearly a year before MTV was created, but Copeland had sensed that video would quickly become an important link between bands and fans.

The idea for MTV was conceived during the music industry recession of the late 1970s. Although record sales were declining, and some were questioning the viability of rock music in the wake of disco, teens had disposable income, and they certainly watched lots of television. The aim of MTV was to provide "visual radio" to a white, middle-class demographic of twelve- to twenty-four-year-olds. Poorly prepared VJs

Nina Blackwood, Mark Goodman, and Martha Quinn hosted this new visual radio station. In many ways, MTV appeared to be an amateur operation. The graphic designs were choppy, the VJs frequently looked ill at ease with the content, and, at least in the early years, many of the music videos were comically bad. Much of MTV's amateurism was by design, though. In reality, the puckish irreverence and low-budget looks of the upstart channel were integral to the aesthetic of MTV from the beginning. John Lack and Robert Pittman, MTV's primary creators and designers, wanted young viewers to believe that anything could happen at any moment.

Combining television with music had been done in the past with shows like *American Bandstand*, *Soul Train*, and *Shindig!*, but MTV's irreverence and youthful energy provided a potent new platform for music promotion. When MTV debuted on August 1, 1981, with The Buggles's "Video Killed the Radio Star" (an English hit from 1979), viewers were already primed for an "all-music channel." By the early 1980s, channels that featured specific content were becoming more common. Nickelodeon, an all-kids network, CNN, an all-news network, and all-movie networks like HBO were already on the air. Furthermore, music videos had become a standard method of promotion in Europe on shows like *Top of the Pops*, *Musikladen*, and *Old Grey Whistle Test*, so MTV immediately looked toward Europe and England for content. Sting recalls this early video era: "When the MTV idea came up, a lot of British bands had these videos, which were instant programming, so The Police had a lot of videos. We were pretty telegenic at the time" ("Video Killed: Sting"). In fact, of the first twenty music videos ever played on MTV, only half were by American-born artists.

By 1982, MTV was still not available in large markets like New York and Los Angeles, and it was apparent that some cable operators were reluctant to carry the channel. This reluctance may be attributed to the limited number of slots for non-local broadcasts and conservative ownerships who were skeptical of the rock-oriented content. In an attempt to improve its availability, MTV launched an innovative promotional campaign employing the slogan, "I want my MTV!" This commercial slogan featured MTV's most popular performers, including the members of The Police, and was in heavy rotation throughout the early 1980s. Sting even integrated the iconic slogan into his background vocals for Dire Straits' "Money for Nothing." This campaign encouraged fans to contact their local cable company to demand MTV, and the strategy worked. By 1983, large markets were open to MTV, and it was available to over 18 million homes.

MTV provided an innovative and powerful form of promotion for popular music, and The Police were in a perfect position to exploit it. They were three good-looking, charismatic, and telegenic musicians who were willing to do anything to promote their music. Furthermore, Sting had already shown an interest in acting and had appeared in the films *Radio On*, *Quadrophenia*, and *Artemis 81*. Miles Copeland certainly took advantage of this new source of promotion. Aside from providing a steady stream of videos from the band, in 1983 he negotiated a deal for MTV to sponsor and promote the Synchronicity Tour. This record-breaking world tour was fantastically successful, and it situated The Police as the biggest band in the world. MTV tirelessly promoted the tour with nonstop news segments, merchandise, fan contests, and live broadcasts. By 1984, The Police and MTV were practically synonymous, and Sting was one of its biggest stars.

PRE-MTV VIDEO PROMOTIONS

Before the arrival of MTV in 1981, and the subsequent realization that music videos could be so important, videos were necessary but neglected promotional tools for English and European bands. Low-budget videos were played in nightclubs or used as substitutes for live performances on music television shows; most musicians and record labels spent little time or money creating a compelling or quality product. In other words, music videos were a necessary marketing tool that did not attract much artistic attention. In some respects, the videos of Derek and Kate Burbidge were a product of that viewpoint. Most of their early videos, including those produced for The Police, were low budget and unrefined. Their videos may appear archaic when compared to the standards of today, but the Burbidges were experienced with the genre and had worked with bands like Queen prior to The Police. In the end, The Police and their management must have been satisfied with the Burbidges' work, because the team directed all the videos for the band through 1982. After their tenure with The Police, the Burbidges would go on to produce videos for AC/DC, The Pretenders, and the Eurythmics.

Most of the Burbidge videos feature live footage of a performance or a sound check. This type of footage was relatively convenient and inexpensive to film because the band was constantly performing. Videos for "Roxanne," "Can't Stand Losing You," and "Message in a Bottle" are largely constructed of live footage interspersed with various backstage antics. During the enacted performance scenes, the band clearly does not take video making seriously. Their mimes are sloppy, Summers looks disinterested, and Stewart Copeland clearly does not know how to depict his job as a drummer in a scene that has no drums. He is frequently relegated to tapping on any object that is available. Copeland laments, "Shooting a video is fine if you're the singer. You just sing into the camera. A guitarist can twang his guitar, but what's the drummer supposed to do? I just have to jerk along with the music, feeling like a dick" (*Everyone Stares*). Copeland's unease with his role in these videos is epitomized in "Walking on the Moon," throughout which he comically taps on rocket boosters because he simply has nothing else to do.

The Burbidges took advantage of the band's continual touring schedule by filming them in exotic tour locations. One example, the video for "So Lonely," was filmed around a Tokyo subway in early 1980. Throughout the video, the band is inexplicably singing into walkie-talkies as Summers struggles to subdue a smirk, and Copeland is tapping on everything he sees. Nevertheless, there is an exotic charm to the street scenes and casual onlookers. More exoticism is apparent in the videos for "Every Little Thing She Does Is Magic" and "Spirits in the Material World," which were filmed in Montserrat in the summer of 1981. Once again, the band was conveniently filmed anywhere they happened to be; in this case, the recording studio. During these scenes, they mime to the song while manipulating studio equipment and maniacally dancing around a small control room. Other scenes feature the band members among the Montserrat populace, who are enjoying the music as well. Like Tokyo, Montserrat provided a colorful and exotic locale that was the perfect counterpart for a lighthearted tune like "Every Little Thing She Does Is Magic."

One of the band's most memorable videos, "Walking on the Moon," took place on October 23, 1979, at the Kennedy Space Center, where the band clearly had permission to do anything they wished. Andy Summers describes what the video shoot was like:

> We have a special pass to see the rockets and spaceships of the 1960s, and we clamber about this old technology that has actually been into space and I think about Dan Dare and the Mekon and *Journey into Space.* We begin the daft process of illustrating the song by miming the lyrics and larking about on giant fins and retro-boosters, etc. This is a couple of years before MTV and the era of solipsistic video. Handheld Super 8 and 16 mm with introspective victim attitudes are still a thing of the future. We are still in the Beatles era of happy, larking-about personality video, and our efforts are based mostly on this alone; our job on camera is to shine. (*One Train Later*, 236)

Indeed, if there is one element that pervades nearly all the Burbidge videos, it is that the band is portrayed as zany, fun loving, youthful, and eccentric. It was clearly an effort to relate to young fans, and in this regard, the Burbidges were masterful. Admittedly, they took a casual approach; the videos are minimally edited, there are few camera angles, the participants are sometimes disinterested or exhausted, and little is offered in terms of visual artistry, but the videos convey a unique energy. As Summers states, the gravitas of video making had not yet arrived, so these videos exemplify the joyousness of a youthful band. This innocence harkens to the early videos of The Beatles and The Monkees, which portray these bands as models of unrestrained youth. Of course, in the case of The Police, it was a manufactured innocence, which would largely disappear when big-budget videos became the norm.

Two Burbidge videos stand out as important contributors to the development of The Police's and Sting's public personas. First, the video for "Don't Stand so Close to Me," filmed in the summer of 1980, is the only video that attempts to offer a literal portrayal of a song. It opens with a young woman, presumably Sting's pupil, trying to attract her teacher's attention. In the video, Sting actually plays two characters, a new wave rocker and a sexy but frazzled teacher. The rocker, who shows off his tanned physique with a sleeveless t-shirt, participates in the customary comical antics but is always centered within the camera shot. Indeed, his blonde hair and striking features are the focal points of the entire video. Later, the more conservative teacher is overtaken by the moment and discards his inhibitions by undressing. Summers explains:

> "Don't Stand so Close to Me" is to be the first single, and we make a
> silly video at a dance school in Clapham in which we prance about in
> black gowns and mortarboards in the already dated conventions of
> pop song videos. I find these video shoots frustrating because they
> seem a too literal translation of the songs. Why, I wonder, can't we
> make a different kind of video, something that has some level of
> ambiguity, a hint of darkness? Something more fucked up. (*One
> Train Later*, 261)

While Summers lamented that these videos could have had more gravitas, the object was not to alienate teenaged viewers; it was to make Sting a sexy rock star. In the video, as Sting disrobes, Summers looks into the camera and begins to smile, but this is no laughing matter; Sting's striking good looks were the greatest marketing asset of the band.

The second video, "Invisible Sun," is an attempt at antiwar activism, which would become an important component of Sting's solo career. Although the lyrics could relate to any war-torn situation, the mention of an ArmaLite weapon (a firearm frequently used by the Provisional Irish Republican Army) hints at which conflict the song really is about. With this in mind, the Burbidges compiled black-and-white footage of Northern Ireland, featuring images of a funeral and a small boy throwing a rock at an armored personnel carrier in the foreground, with silhouettes of the band fading in and out. These powerful images were controversial enough that the BBC banned the video. Although the controversy increased interest in the song, the video was no hollow publicity stunt. The band was certainly aware of various worldwide humanitarian crises. Copeland's childhood home in Beirut was under siege by Israeli troops during the recording and promotion of *Ghost in the Machine*, and they all were clearly familiar with the turmoil in Northern Ireland. Summers comments on the BBC censorship:

> "Invisible Sun" is the first single off this album, and the video is
> immediately banned by the BBC for political content they don't want
> to show on the grounds that it is too controversial. Once again the
> institution shows that it is living in the Stone Age and with a double

standard. Our video contains no violent imagery but shows kids in Belfast—the lives of people in Northern Ireland and what they are subjected to. The BBC shows violent newsreels all the time, but when the same subject matter is expressed artistically they prefer to ban it—and by doing so promote it. (*One Train Later*, 301)

"Invisible Sun" is by far the most artistically gratifying of all the Burbidge videos. Furthermore, it hints at Sting's future role as a humanitarian. Throughout the 1980s and 1990s, Sting's worldwide persona was not only as a pop music superstar but also as a representative for various humanitarian causes, like preserving the Amazon rain forest. This is still an important aspect of Sting's public image, and it has defined him through much of his career.

GODLEY AND CREME

Kevin Godley and Lol Creme met in the late 1950s while attending a Manchester art school. The two were in a variety of bands throughout the 1960s, culminating with the band Hotlegs, with Graham Gouldman and Eric Stewart, in 1970. In 1972, they changed their band name to 10cc and produced their first minor hit, "Donna." In 1975, 10cc had their biggest hit to date, "I'm Not in Love"; nonetheless, both Godley and Creme decided to leave the band in order to explore their art rock tendencies with the album *Consequences* in 1976. Although *Consequences* was a commercial and critical failure, in 1979 Godley and Creme had two minor hits from their third album, *Freeze Frame*. Coincidently, this album was recorded at Nigel Gray's Surrey Sound Studios, the same studio where The Police recorded *Outlandos d'Amour* and *Reggatta de Blanc*. One of the hits from *Freeze Frame* was "An Englishman in New York" (no relation to the Sting song of the same name), for which Godley and Creme created an innovative video featuring a bizarre mix of live action and puppetry. Following the success garnered by the video for "An Englishman in New York," directing music videos became a viable creative and commercial outlet for the duo.

In July 1981, Godley and Creme began production on a video for Duran Duran's "Girls on Film." Although the video was created nearly simultaneously with the launching of MTV, Godley and Creme had not anticipated that it would ever be broadcast on mainstream media outlets. As a result, the video for "Girls on Film" features nudity and highly provocative sexual situations. Kevin Godley explains, "Movie videos were being played in a different kind of environment. They were being played away from broadcast mediums, so what was possible didn't have censorship written on it. You could actually show stuff that you didn't have to worry about too much" ("Video Killed: Duran Duran"). Godley and Creme expected the video to be played in nightclubs or on cable channels like Playboy, not on a music channel available to millions of middle-class homes. Ultimately, the video was edited for MTV and banned by the BBC, but the controversy fueled interest in Duran Duran and, of course, in Godley and Creme.

By 1983, MTV was growing at a record pace, and music videos were becoming more sophisticated. Artists like Talking Heads, Michael Jackson, and David Bowie were creating compelling videos featuring sophisticated graphic designs, large sets, and expensive makeup and costumes. By this time, The Police was one of the biggest bands in the world and inexorably tied to MTV, so they needed to produce quality videos that were equal to those of their peers. Sadly, The Police had outgrown the puckish videos of the Burbidges, so they hired Godley and Creme to direct their last four videos. Godley and Creme's reputation as innovative video producers and as competent musicians made them attractive to The Police. "Why did we choose Kevin and Lol? First and foremost, they were musicians. They had a visual sense as well as a musical sense. I felt we could have a rapport with people who were already musicians, and they could understand what we were doing and give us the extra visual impact of storytelling on film," Sting recalls ("Video Killed: Sting"). Indeed, the duo provided remarkable ideas for the videos for The Police. Because of their directorship, the videos for "Every Breath You Take" and "Wrapped around Your Finger" are among the most enduring and iconic videos of the 1980s.

"Every Breath You Take" became The Police's biggest hit. It was at the top of the *Billboard* Hot 100 singles chart for two months in 1983 and was one of the most popular songs of the year. Its distinctive video unquestionably helped fuel this popularity. Godley and Creme were reluctant to provide a literal interpretation of the song, choosing rather to create a simple atmosphere reminiscent of the film noir movies of the 1940s, with a black-and-white background that evoked a smoky jazz club. Sting was particularly supportive of this interpretation: "It was a very simple video. Stark black-and-white colors. I always like black and white because I'm color blind. I always think there's more information in black and white film than there is in color film. . . . It had a drama to it. There was a sense of irony about it" ("Video Killed: Sting").

The video for "Wrapped around Your Finger" is equally compelling. In it, the band is surrounded with hundreds of lighted candles, configured in a maze-like pattern. As usual, Sting is featured, and he dances among the candles, eventually knocking many of them down as he exits. Once again, this visual depiction has little to do with the lyrics, but its ethereal appearance makes it particularly memorable.

Beyond the costumes, expensive sets, and visual effects, the videos for "Every Breath You Take" and "Wrapped around Your Finger" mark an important shift of aesthetic. These videos utilize the band members in dual roles. Naturally, they play the role of musicians, holding and playing their instruments, but they also become actors. In the case of "Every Breath You Take," they are jazz musicians in a smoky nightclub. Sting, in the video for "Wrapped around Your Finger," never plays his bass; instead, he is a dancing Svengali. In other words, these videos promote The Police beyond the level of simply musicians; they are pop culture icons.

STING AND *BRING ON THE NIGHT*

When Sting became a solo artist, Miles Copeland continued as his manager. Copeland had proved that his fearless managerial style was effective, and although Sting was an internationally known figure, solo success was not a given. When Sting began his official push for solo stardom in 1985, Copeland used the same strategies as when he promoted The Police with *Around the World* by creating a video media event to coincide with the release of Sting's first solo album, *The Dream of the Blue Turtles*.

Michael Apted was hired to direct the video, titled *Bring on the Night*, but unlike the Burbidges or Godley and Creme, he was already an acclaimed film director. Apted was best known for his contributions to the *Up* television series and was a well-respected film director of movies like *Agatha*, *Coal Miner's Daughter*, and *Gorky Park*. His job was to provide a video documentary of the launch of Sting's solo career and presumably his new band. The film begins with scenes of Paris that gradually shift to the French countryside and the Château de Courson. This seventeenth-century château, just outside of Paris, exemplified the venerableness of French culture, and it certainly reflected Sting's new maturity. As the camera approaches, the sounds of Sting and his band emanate from an inner hall. This sophisticated scenery is an unusual opening for a popular music documentary. Sting surely could have picked more modern surroundings from which to film his inaugural rehearsals and concert; it certainly would have evoked something far different if it had been filmed in New York City, London, or even Los Angeles. Instead, Sting and Miles Copeland chose a more exotic venue, a marketing approach reminiscent of the Burbidge's approach to *Around the World*. Keep in mind that Sting was nearly thirty-five years old, and his music no longer targeted teenagers. His listener base had shifted beyond the teenaged demographic who enjoyed The Police just a few years earlier. In choosing such an exotic location, Sting acknowledged that while he remained an international entertainer, as he was with The Police, he was also creating a new, more mature, public persona.

In order to sustain viewer interest, Apted incorporated a number of narratives into *Bring on the Night*. First, the issue of Sting's viability as a solo artist is discussed throughout the film. Although it seems inconceivable for an artist such as Sting to fail, Apted interjects concerns from many of Sting's closest friends. Kim Turner states in the film, "He's in competition with probably the greatest act in history, The Police. That's the risk." Even Miles Copeland adds a practical concern, "I don't think the risk is necessarily in the music he's chosen. The risk is being only on his own, where there's no cocoon. Every interview has to be done by him, whereas in The Police, he'd only do a quarter of the interviews because the others would carry the bulk of it. Everything now is Sting. The pressure is the important difference between this situation and the one he was in with The Police." Although these kinds of concerns make for good movie making, after hearing the quality of music Sting was creating and seeing the earnestness he was putting into his post-Police career, it is difficult to believe anyone had serious doubts about his success.

The second narrative addresses the status of Sting's musicians. The question of equality is posed to Sting's new band: is this really an egalitarian group of artists or a collection of backing musicians? The answer is somewhere in the middle. Of course, Sting is the star. He has interviewed and auditioned every member, he has full creative and monetary control, and he does not share writing credits with any of the other musicians. On the other hand, his bandmates clearly participate in the live-music-making process. For example, Sting gives his band ample time to solo during certain tunes, at times making the musicians an integral part of the musical fabric. For instance, Kenny Kirkland's piano solo on the album version of "Bring on the Night/When the World Is Running Down" has become such an essential part of the tune that subsequent Sting pianists have quoted it on tour. In the end, these musicians were very experienced in the ways of the music business, and they surely knew that they were not on equal footing with Sting, but they played along anyway.

Lastly, Apted touches on issues relating to race and Sting's entirely African American band. In the mid-1980s, this was a particularly sensitive topic. In its early days, MTV had been criticized for marginalizing African American performers, because so few black videos were placed on heavy rotation. And the most common criticism of Sting and The Police was that they had "stolen" ethnic styles like reggae and had profited greatly. Moreover, Sting had a tendency to be aloof and erudite when dealing with the press, so they were sometimes eager to criticize his artistic and marketing decisions. In the film, Sting confronts any criticism by blatantly stating, "Black musicians are not really given the opportunity to be heard on white radio or in white publications. And it's just as bad the other way. This band, being made up racially as it is, is an open challenge to that system." Indeed, it was uncommon to see a white superstar with an all-African American band, but there rarely appears to be any real tension within the band. During one of the film's interviews, Branford Marsalis sidesteps the racial issue altogether and targets cultural differences as the possible source of any controversy: "The major thing was the social barrier, of him being British and white and us being American and black." Marsalis goes on to describe linguistic and social differences between the two cultures, but these differences are minor and not necessarily framed by race.

Michael Apted would eventually regret the promotion of *Bring on the Night*. He laments that the film was not more connected to the hit album: "We didn't want the film to look like an MTV version of the album but realize now we should have used the LP to sell the film. We avoided it. We underestimated the drawing power of the album" (Beck). Regrets aside, *Bring on the Night* was successful enough that Sting quickly became an international superstar.

STING AND JAGUAR

Surprisingly, Sting was remarkably hands off when it came to video production. He deftly managed his persona in terms of tours, merchandise, media events, promotions, and charity engagements, yet Sting did not have much interest in music videos: "My approach to videos was to leave it to the directors. I'm interested in music" ("Video Killed: Sting"). This is not to say that Sting didn't care about his video image, but he put his full trust in his producers and directors. "I'm not a visual artist, never could be. I'm completely confident that if you choose the right person to work with, they will make it work. That's very trusting of me, but it's served me well. Choose the right people, and they do the best thing without me just getting in the way" ("Video Killed: Sting"). Considering Sting's hands-off attitude, it is ironic that one of his music videos would spur an important late-career renaissance.

On October 10, 1999, the video for "Desert Rose," the second single from Sting's *Brand New Day* album, was shot in the desert outside of Las Vegas. The video features Sting being chauffeured in a Jaguar S-Type sedan by a masked woman. He is driven through the desert, soon arriving at a concert of Cheb Mami, who is surrounded by dancing women, DJs, and various provocative scenes. Mami, who is prominently featured throughout the song, was a popular Algerian raï singer. Raï, an Algerian folk music originating in the 1930s, contains a mixture of Spanish, French, African, and various Arabic musical styles. Consequently, Mami's raï-inspired vocal timbre and phrasing lends a distinctly non-Western sound to "Desert Rose."

Of course, Sting's career had been framed by utilizing exotic styles like raï, so it was characteristic of him to use such an unusual musical sound within a pop song. Additionally, Miles Copeland's record label, Ark 21, had been established in 1997 to distribute world music to Western markets, and the talented and telegenic Cheb Mami was on Copeland's artist roster. It is doubtful, though, that the unusual "Desert

Rose" would have gotten much radio play in the West without an innovative marketing strategy, and this video provided that opportunity.

Once Copeland had seen the video, featuring not only Sting but a Jaguar sedan, he approached Jaguar's advertising agency with a proposition: "If you will make the commercial look like an ad for my record, I'll give you the rights for free. Just as long as you have a big enough TV campaign to make this worthwhile" (Donaton, 141). A&M records had provided $1.8 million to promote and record a video for *Brand New Day*, but Jaguar had an advertising budget of $18.9 million, which included a massive number of television commercials. Moreover, the Jaguar commercial was essentially the original music video with a bit of added narrative: "Everyone dreams of becoming a rock star. What then do rock stars dream of?" The only mention of the Jaguar brand name appears at the end of the commercial. Prior to the commercial's release, interest in "Desert Rose" was minimal—"we had zero Top 40 stations"—but it ignited interest in the song and eventually led to the sale of over 6 million copies of *Brand New Day*.

This innovative collaboration between art and advertising led to many more sponsored promotions. Jimmy Iovine, the chairman of Interscope/Geffen/A&M, comments on how significant Copeland's idea was: "Because he took an artist with the credibility of Sting and took a gigantic step forward. And a lot of what you're seeing right now is because of Sting and Jaguar and Miles. We learned a lot from them" (Donaton, 138). Iovine is correct; corporate sponsors would be integral to music promotion in the future, and Sting's own future tours would be promoted by corporate sponsors like Clear Channel, Compaq Computers, and Xerox. When The Police reunited in 2007, of course, they were sponsored by Best Buy.

5

STING IN THE AGE OF GLOBAL ACTIVISM

Today, concerts and recordings benefitting the victims of natural disasters or political atrocities are common, but that has not always been the case. The age of global musical activism began in the 1980s, at a time when pop music performers were achieving unprecedented popularity due to the expansion of media outlets like MTV. More than any other type of media, MTV expanded the image of the pop music star in the 1980s. It provided teenaged viewers a continuous stream of visual representations of pop performers, which launched them to the highest levels of international popularity. Portrayals of these performers in musical videos ranged from the promiscuous to the heroic, thus creating dramatic personas that defined the public images of these artists for decades. Furthermore, music videos were not relegated to the fringes of the broadcast world; they were sometimes premiered as media events on prime-time television networks. By the late 1980s, music videos had become an essential tool in creating the international images of popular music performers. In addition to music videos, MTV broadcasted live concerts, providing even the most provincial viewers an opportunity to see and experience live performances of the biggest pop stars in the world. MTV also integrated news and interviews within its programming, providing a real and visceral look into the personal lives of performers, beyond what fans could get from just a magazine. This level of access created a generation of internationally beloved artists with unrivalled popularity like Michael Jackson, Sting, Prince, Madonna, Phil Collins, Bono, and Bruce Springsteen. Moreover, much of

MTV's video content came from Europe and, of course, England. These overseas performers presented new cultural perspectives to American audiences, and for the first time, millions of American teens were regularly listening to socially conscious artists like Martika ("Toy Soldiers"), Dire Straits ("Brothers in Arms"), Depeche Mode ("The Landscape Is Changing"), The Clash ("Rock the Casbah"), Peter Gabriel ("Biko" and "Games without Frontiers"), and U2 ("Mothers of the Disappeared" and "Sunday Bloody Sunday"). The international popularity and visibility of these artists, fueled by MTV, created a type of "cultural capital," which artists used to promote their own humanitarian causes. Of course, cultural capital could only be effective if audiences were receptive, and in the 1980s, they undoubtedly were. The combination of socially conscious artists with a responsive and young audience created a generation of unparalleled global activism.

The Police were certainly a socially conscious band, and by the time they broke apart, they had created a sizable repertoire of tunes based on a variety of social issues: they addressed war and nuclear proliferation with "Bombs Away," "Invisible Sun," and "When the World Is Running Down, You Make the Best of What's Still Around," they acknowledged economic disparity in "Driven to Tears" and "One World (Not Three)," and they critiqued governmental abuse with "Murder by Numbers." Copeland and Summers certainly had a great deal of creative input with these songs, but Sting was the true compositional force in the band. In some ways, Sting may have been situating himself as a global activist while he was still a member of The Police, and after his tenure, he became one of the world's best-known activists. Among his numerous causes were Amnesty International's charity events and tours, Bob Geldof's various activist projects, and his own charity, the Rainforest Foundation. Sting's immersion into activism coincided with the rise of global activism in the 1980s. In fact, the history of this activism is inexorably tied to Sting's personal story of advocacy and involvement.

Of course, there were humanitarian benefits before the 1980s. One of the earliest and best known is George Harrison's Concert for Bangladesh in 1971. This was actually a two-concert event which took place in one day at New York City's Madison Square Garden. The concerts were created to raise awareness and funds for the victims of atrocities relating to the Bangladesh Liberation War. In 1979, Musicians United for

Safe Energy (MUSE) performed five shows at Madison Square Garden to protest the use of nuclear energy after Three Mile Island. Later in 1979, the Concerts for the People of Kampuchea, featuring Queen, The Clash, The Who, The Pretenders, and Elvis Costello, among others, took place at the Hammersmith Odeon in London to raise money and awareness for war-torn Cambodia. All of these concerts were worthy endeavors, but they did not capture the interest of millions around the world, nor did they generate the breathtaking sums and attention of later campaigns.

Among the most important of the early benefits was one presented by Amnesty International. Amnesty was founded in 1961 by English lawyer Peter Beneson. Upon reading an article about two Portuguese students who had been sentenced to seven years in prison for toasting freedom, Beneson formed Amnesty International to spur action against human rights abusers, to conduct human rights research, and to demand justice for people whose rights had been violated. Today, Amnesty has more than 3 million members and agencies in sixty-eight countries. It is regarded as one of the most influential and powerful human rights organizations in the world, and much of this success may be attributed to its innovative fund-raising campaigns. One of these first campaigns was A Poke in the Eye (With a Sharp Stick), a benefit conceived by television and radio personality Martin Lewis and Monty Python's John Cleese. As Lewis explains, Cleese was particularly important to the project:

> He was very keen to support Amnesty at a time that human rights wasn't a topic that most people talked about . . . it usually got buried on page 17 of the serious, quality newspapers, and very few people had even heard of Amnesty. John Cleese was aware of the organization, and he sent them a donation. Amnesty responded by saying, "We greatly appreciate your gift. Is there any way that you could perhaps do a little something more to help us?" (Ragogna)

Lewis knew that "star power" was a vital component of fund-raising, and others would expand on his ideas into the 1980s. This particular benefit consisted of three performances at Her Majesty's Theatre, London, in April 1976, and it featured some of the greatest comedians of the day such as John Cleese, Graham Chapman, and Carol Cleveland, among many others. A recording of the concerts was sold as *A Poke in the Eye (With a Sharp Stick)*, and a film titled *Pleasure at Her Majesty's* was also released. The show and its subsequent audio and video releases were successful enough that in 1977 a second show, titled The Mermaid Frolics, took place.

In 1979, a third benefit show, The Secret Policeman's Ball, incorporated music into the program for the first time. The Who's Pete Townshend, who was asked to provide music as a contrast to the comedic skits, performed acoustic versions of "Pinball Wizard," "Drowned," and "Won't Get Fooled Again" (with John Williams). These poignant acoustic renditions were a hit with viewers and listeners and, according to Martin Lewis, influenced MTV's *Unplugged* series: "Pete told me recently that John Sykes and Bill Flanagan (executives at MTV and VH1) had been very clear to him that MTV's Unplugged had been inspired by what Pete had done at The Secret Policeman's Ball " (Ragogna).

The following benefit, The Secret Policeman's Other Ball, took place over a series of nights in September 1981 and featured many more musicians: Eric Clapton, Phil Collins, Jeff Beck, Donovan, and Sting. Sting, appearing without The Police, performed "Roxanne," "Message in a Bottle," and Bob Dylan's "I Shall Be Released," which was backed by The Secret Police, an all-star band comprised of the night's musical performers. Why did Sting perform these songs instead of his more activist tunes like "Driven to Tears" or "Invisible Sun?" Sting realized early on that his audiences wanted to hear his hits, and "Roxanne" and "Message in a Bottle" were surely his two biggest hits at the time. "Invisible Sun" had only just been released, so most listeners probably were not familiar with it. "I Shall Be Released" served as the finale and was led by Sting, who was not only the dominant figure in the finale but arguably the prevailing performer of the night. This performance attests that, even at this early stage, Sting was moving beyond his teenaged fans, as Chris Connelly confirms: "'Message in a Bottle' does miss the phaser wizardry of Police guitarist Andy Summers, but Sting's booming tenor delivers a 'Roxanne' so brimming with brio it outstrips the original. The best rock vocalist these days? Yes" (67). Sting's presence, both as a global musical icon and as an activist, was taking shape. The importance of these performances cannot be overstated; not only did Sting know very little about Amnesty International before The Secret Policeman's Other Ball, but he shared the stage with another performer who would prove to be a force in global activism, Bob Geldof.

BAND AID

Bob Geldof was known as the outspoken lead singer of The Boomtown Rats. The Boomtown Rats, whose name was inspired by a gang in Woody Guthrie's "Bound for Glory," formed in 1975 in Dun Laoghaire, Ireland. By 1978, the band had its first number one hit with "Rat Trap," a song about a young man who feels trapped in his small town. On a side note, "Rat Trap" was one of the first hits for legendary producer Robert Mutt Lange, who would go on to produce songs for a variety of artists from Shania Twain to Maroon 5. The Boomtown Rats had their biggest hit with "I Don't Like Mondays" in 1979. Although the title may appear lighthearted, the narrative is inspired by Brenda Spencer, a sixteen-year-old California woman who killed a principal and a custodian at a local elementary school. After the shootings, Spencer proclaimed that the reason for the killings was simply, she "didn't like Mondays."

Although The Boomtown Rats released albums throughout the early 1980s, the band never duplicated the remarkable success of "I Don't Like Mondays," and endured a slow slide into obscurity. In late 1984, while watching a BBC documentary by Michael Buerk on famine-stricken Ethiopia, Geldof was inspired to raise money by recording a charity-minded tune. He initially thought he could write and produce the song by himself but soon changed his mind:

> I was just startled by it. Any sort of notions of records, sales, career and crap like that just disappeared. It demanded a response, and I thought, "I know, I'll write a song and the Rats can do it." Of course, immediately, "What's the point of that, we can't even get a really good song going." (*Band Aid*)

Geldof was pessimistic for good reason; he and his band were no longer hit makers, and nothing they wrote was likely to generate much interest or revenue: "We were alienated from our record company. We were alienated from our audience . . . I couldn't do it as a solo artist. I really had very little confidence in my abilities" (*Band Aid*). Possibly taking inspiration from his work with Martin Lewis and The Secret Policeman's Other Ball years earlier, Geldof concluded, "I knew that if I wrote a song, it wouldn't sell. So I needed to get people I knew to sing it" (Lynskey 378). The next day, Geldof called his wife, Paula Yates, a

British television personality and writer, who happened to be interviewing Midge Ure. Coincidentally, Ure had also been a part of The Secret Policeman's Other Ball in 1981 and had shared a microphone with Geldof during the finale.

Midge Ure, a gifted multi-instrumentalist, singer, and producer, had been in a variety of bands but was best known for his work with the new wave band, Ultravox. Unlike Geldof, Ure was approaching the peak of his popularity in 1984. Earlier in the year, Ultravox had a top-five hit with "Dancing with Tears in My Eyes." Ure was obviously aware of protest-related media events; "Dancing with Tears in My Eyes" was accompanied by a video depicting a nuclear engineer running home to his family upon discovering that an atomic explosion was imminent.

Therefore, it was opportune that Ure was in Newcastle appearing on the television show *The Tube*, hosted by Paula Yates, at the time of Geldof's call. Geldof asked Yates who was on the show, and she told him it was Ure; Ure was put on the telephone and was instantly receptive to Geldof's idea: "We chatted and he asked if I'd seen the documentary that had just gone out on BBC television about the problems in Ethiopia. He wanted to do something, and would I help. I said, 'Of course, I would.' So we got together a couple of days later and started throwing ideas around" (Ure interview). Both men knew that the benefit song had to be available by Christmas, so the arduous task of cowriting the single began immediately; said Geldof, "I went home with my little Casio keyboard on my kitchen table and came up with what I thought was a real Christmasy tune" (*Band Aid*). With only fragments of the song ready, Geldof began asking every performer he knew, and some he did not know, to participate. One of the first calls he made was to Sting. As Geldof had known Sting long before The Secret Policeman's Other Ball, he knew that Sting was open to charity engagements. Geldof also knew that Sting was a talented and disciplined singer. In fact, Geldof and Ure asked him to sing the primary melodies and harmonies of the tune at Ure's studio before the official recording session on November 25:

> Sting sang his harmony parts—"and there won't be snow in Africa at Christmas time" and "the bitter sting of tears"—to my guide vocal. But when we changed it, whoever it was that sang the line—Glenn Gregory, Bono or George Michael—Sting's harmony still fitted perfectly. It was electric. (Ure, 136)

The recording session was the remarkable product of media savvy, benefaction, talent, professionalism, and luck. Through dogged determination and aggressive arm twisting, Geldof gathered some of the best-known British musicians in world, including Phil Collins, Paul Young, Simon Le Bon, Bono, George Michael, Boy George, and Jody Watley. Geldof was not particularly known as an activist, so his requests surprised some artists. Bono received Geldof's call while in Germany: "All I remembered was having rows with Geldof about how he thought pop music and rock 'n' roll should stay away from politics and agitprop, be sexy, fun, mischievous. So it was odd to get a call from Geldof to talk about Africa" (Lynskey, 379). Keep in mind that these were not only the biggest stars of Britain, but also the largest egos, so Geldof's greatest challenge may have been simply to get everyone to work together. During the recording session, Sting confirmed the challenges brought about by massive egos: "A very interesting kind of chemistry went on. At first, their very fragile egos walked through the door and I thought if it was going to be alright, but there's a lovely spirit. Everybody's mucking in and singing together. It's great" (*Do They Know It's Christmas*). One way that Geldof may have kept his artists in line was the presence of the press. The morning of the session, while Geldof and Ure dramatically stood outside Sarm Studios waiting for the performers to arrive, reporters, photographers, and videographers gathered. As the performers arrived in various limousines (Sting arrived on foot but may have been dropped off a block away), the press acted as if it was a Hollywood red carpet event. Geldof had clearly given certain media members full access, and they documented most of the evening. If an artist was too resistant or simply complained too much, it would have been front page material. Months later, Geldof would use the same kind of press leverage while organizing Live Aid. Nevertheless, a gathering of such large stars on short notice was a miraculous feat. "It had been a monumental day. There was never one second of rancorous feeling. People wanted to hang around and talk to each other, suggest things. Some were in awe of each other's abilities. Inside that room had been the single greatest collection of contemporary musicians in British history," Geldof recalls (Geldof and Vallely, 289).

Amazingly, Band Aid's "Do They Know It's Christmas?" was released on November 29, just days after it was recorded. Geldof asked the visual artist Peter Blake, who designed the iconic target and arrow logo for The Who as well as the cover for The Beatles' album *Sgt. Pepper's Lonely Hearts Club Band,* to provide the cover art. Blake created a collage of various Victorian Christmas scenes, bluntly juxtaposed with a photo of two starving African children. The record label and distributors released the album at little or no cost, and consumers loved it. Geldof's promise that all merchandise, sales, publishing, and performance contributions would go to famine relief awakened the goodwill in millions of consumers, and it quickly became the fastest-selling single of all time in the United Kingdom (a record that would be surpassed by Elton John's "Candle in the Wind 1997"). More than one million copies were sold in the first week, and many consumers bought more than one copy, just to support the cause.

Aside from the obvious charitable merits of the single, "Do They Know It's Christmas?" is simply a compelling song. The various vocalists brilliantly interpret the sometimes morose lyrics, while chimes remind the listeners that this is indeed a Christmas song, and the canonical choral finale combines the communal setting with a tuneful melody. In short, the song is meaningful, but it is also catchy and fun. Sting comments, "There was a charming naivety about this song. A more sophisticated song would not have worked. It had to be a kind of Christmas carol, nursery rhyme, simple, idealistic vision, and that's exactly what it was" (*Band Aid*). Adding to the song's appeal, it was a challenge for listeners to guess which performers were singing at any one time. This element of the listening experience was unique, and it added to the novelty of the single. Also, the music video featured popular artists who had never been seen together before, and particularly for teenage fans, seeing idols among other idols was indeed exciting. Because of his high profile in the media and his boisterous manner, Geldof ultimately was the face of Band Aid, but he admits that the credit for crafting and producing the single should go to Ure:

> He made the record. That's really it. Midge made that a hit record. There's no question of that. A lot of the ideas are excellent. It's so full of foreboding, and there's so clearly an African sort of thing going on . . . how did he get that out of the crap I played him? I had absolutely nothing to contribute to the record. I want to state that here and now. The record is his. ("Making of Band Aid")

For Sting, Band Aid was an important milestone in his career. The Synchronicity Tour had ended in March 1984, and he had spent September and October filming *The Bride*. He was also preparing for his solo debut in 1985, but his schedule allowed him to comfortably attend the recording sessions for Band Aid. Furthermore, his added vocal tracks, his relationship with Geldof, and his top-tier status among his peers resulted in prominence during the video and on the album. Even Simon Le Bon admitted that it was an honor to work with him, "I actually had Sting standing next to me when I recorded my bit. Rather than make me feel nervous and uncomfortable, I took great comfort from that. I was very proud to be on the microphone next to Sting" (*Band Aid*). On video, Sting's striking looks and serious demeanor separated him from his peers, but more importantly, the cultural gravitas of Band Aid set the stage for his more mature persona.

The unprecedented success of Band Aid inspired like-minded singles from around the world. In Latin America, all-star groups Project Hermanos and Nordeste Já recorded *Cantaré Cantarás (I Will Sing, You Will Sing)* and *Chega de Mágoa* in 1985. In Germany, *Nackt im Wind* was performed by Band für Afrika, and the French supergroup Chanteurs sans frontières released *Ethiopie*. Even heavy metal artists contributed to the cause with *Stars* by the metal group Hear 'n Aid. In the following years, Band Aid was remade with a new crop of contemporary artists as Band Aid II (1989), Band Aid 20 (2004), and Band Aid 30 (2014). Certainly the best known of these Band Aid–inspired singles was "We Are the World," by USA for Africa. After seeing what Geldof had accomplished, Harry Belafonte and Lionel Richie's manager, Ken Kragen, gathered some of the biggest American pop stars for a recording session at A&M Studios in Los Angeles on January 28, 1985. "We Are the World," written by Richie and Michael Jackson, featured an all-star cast of Stevie Wonder, Kenny Rogers, Diana Ross, Bruce Springsteen, Cyndi Lauper, Michael Jackson, Huey Lewis, and many more. The funds generated by "We Are the World" quadrupled those of Band Aid and provided an American contribution to global activism. In fact, America would also play a prominent role during Geldof's next venture, Live Aid.

LIVE AID

The success of Band Aid emboldened Bob Geldof to move on to the next stage of his plan, which was to organize a globally televised concert. In early March of 1985, after fulfilling touring obligations with The Boomtown Rats, Geldof began assembling a team of producers, managers, and technical advisers who could assist him with an even grander event than Band Aid. Geldof's idea was an all-star concert, presumably based in London, which would be broadcast around the world. As the plan progressed, Geldof's ambitions grew larger, and a broader network of concerts was conceived. Even for Geldof, this was an extraordinarily ambitious idea. Harvey Goldsmith, an English promoter and manager, was one of the central figures in organizing Live Aid and had reservations about the event from the beginning: "I basically told him to fuck off at first because I thought he was being ridiculous. . . . Basically, everything he said he wanted to do, I said, 'you can't.' That was our starting point" ("Against All Odds").

Goldsmith's reluctance was well founded. There were formidable logistical obstacles to Live Aid. To begin with, a live global broadcast in 1985 posed sizable technological challenges. Many of those challenges were referred to another member of Geldof's team, Michael C. Mitchell. Mitchell was the president of Worldwide Sports and Entertainment, which had been involved in the broadcast of the 1984 Olympic Games. He knew that Live Aid, which demanded the organization and synchronization of multiple live performances, would dwarf the technological demands of the previous year's Olympic broadcast:

> We were literally laughed out of all three networks' offices. In the Olympics, we used two satellites, one feed, one location to a world feed. Live Aid: sixteen satellites, eight locations, all interactive feed for sixteen hours. In today's terms, it would be like saying, "Let's do a concert on the moon." ("Against All Odds")

Nevertheless, Geldof's team worked with BBC, ABC, and MTV to broadcast the concerts throughout the day on July 13, 1985.

Another sizable challenge to Geldof was booking artists. Although Band Aid and USA for Africa had been unqualified successes, there was reluctance among many performers, particularly the American contingent, to be associated with a potentially controversial charity event.

Questions of how much money would go directly to victims introduced a possibility that contributing artists could be associated with a potential public scandal. There were also scheduling and logistical issues involved. Some artists were asked to alter their lucrative tour schedules. Some artists, such as The Who and Led Zeppelin, had not performed together for years and were surely out of practice. Moreover, most of the performers participating in Live Aid were asked to shoulder the financial burden of personnel and equipment transportation, rehearsal time, lodging, food, and innumerable other expenses. It was a lot for Geldof to ask, so he used the media as a tool of persuasion.

In one of the boldest moves in the history of popular culture, Bob Geldof organized a press conference at Wembley Stadium to announce the artists scheduled to perform at Live Aid before the negotiations were finalized. Some of the artists like Sting and U2 had agreed early on, but many of the performers that Geldof announced as "confirmed" had only agreed on principle. Nevertheless, he announced commitments by Dire Straits, Kris Kristofferson, Alison Moyet, and Queen, knowing that any agreements had been informal at best, but in hopes that the negative publicity associated with backing out of Live Aid would leverage reluctant artists to participate:

> I realized that talking on the phone to musicians was one thing, but unless it was in the papers, they weren't going to commit. If you look at the original list that was announced, and at who actually appeared, you'll see what was going on. Bryan Ferry rang me up and said, "Listen, I haven't agreed to this," and I said, "Well, it's cool, Bryan, if you want to pull out, that's fine. I just have to go out and announce it." Of course, really, he couldn't. (Tannenbaum, "Bob Geldof," 76)

For various reasons, renowned artists like Michael Jackson, Boy George, Billy Joel, Stevie Wonder, and Bruce Springsteen could not perform at Live Aid, but Geldof's blunt powers of persuasion worked on most of those he asked. As Sting has stated, "you don't say 'no' to Bob Geldof very easily." Ultimately, Geldof was not interested in the artists themselves; instead, he was looking for the publicity that they attracted. "I could give a fuck if they do it or not. All I'm interested in is that they go onstage and half of the world phones in with their dollar or their pound note or their franc or their ruble" (Fricke, "Bob Geldof,"

18). Indeed, the popularity of the Live Aid performers made it a once-in-a-lifetime global event.

The two primary concerts were held simultaneously at London's Wembley Stadium and John F. Kennedy Stadium in Philadelphia. The London concert began first with a proclamation from BBC broadcaster Richard Skinner: "It's 12 noon in London, 7 AM in Philadelphia, and around the world, it's time for Live Aid. Wembley welcomes their Royal Highnesses, the Prince and Princess of Wales." Following this announcement, Prince Charles and Princess Diana entered to a royal fanfare, followed by "God Save the Queen." From the outset, Geldof worked to make Live Aid a grand historic spectacle, and the appearance of royalty was an important element to the proceedings. Diana and Charles's work with charities, and, of course, their status, provided an unquestionable historical gravitas to the event.

A large placard placed over Wembley's stage, reading "Feed the World July 13 1985 at Wembley Stadium," signified what Geldof was attempting to achieve with Live Aid. To begin with, fund-raising was the primary aim of Live Aid, and Geldof did not want any viewer or attendee to forget it. "Feed the World" was a clear statement of intent, and he knew this constant reminder would work. To aid in fund-raising, over 300 telephone lines were provided to take contributions. Geldof himself even appeared onscreen to plead for more telephone donations: "Get on the phone and take the money out of your pocket. Don't go to the pub first, please stay in, and give us the money. There are people dying now! So give me the money." His appeals worked; Live Aid raised over $250 million for African famine aid. Secondly, Geldof also reinforced his charitable pleas with constant reminders that Live Aid was historical and special, and the date above the Wembley stage reminded everyone that this day would be remembered. Indeed, the event was historical in viewership and attendance, with 72,000 attendees at Wembley Stadium and 90,000 at JFK Stadium, as well as live and taped concerts from Australia, Germany, Austria, Norway, Japan, the Soviet Union, and Yugoslavia. ABC broadcast three hours in the United States, while MTV provided all-day coverage, but commercial breaks resulted in some songs being edited from the broadcast. Of course, British viewers were offered the BBC broadcast. The London show began at noon and concluded at 10 PM, while the JFK Stadium concert began at 9 AM and concluded at 11 PM. Appropriately, the program at Wembley ended with an all-star version of "Do They Know It's Christmas?," and the concert at JFK Stadium concluded with "We Are the World." An estimated 1.5 billion viewers watched the various broadcasts from more than a hundred countries.

Geldof emphasized the grandness of the event by orchestrating a number of memorable moments. Some were planned, and some were simply products of the day. One of the most remarkable events of Live Aid featured Phil Collins. In the afternoon, Collins performed two of his biggest hits at the time, "Against All Odds (Take a Look at Me Now)" and "In the Air Tonight," at Wembley. Immediately after this performance, he dramatically boarded a helicopter that shuttled him to Heathrow Airport, then took the Concorde to Philadelphia. After arriving at JFK Stadium, he played drums with Eric Clapton, sang a solo set, and appeared on drums with the reunited Led Zeppelin. Unfortunately, neither Jimmy Page nor Robert Plant was pleased with the performance, and rebroadcast of their portion of Live Aid has been discouraged. Still, historical reunions were a notable part of Live Aid. Not only did Led Zeppelin reform, but The Who and Black Sabbath reunited as well.

Geldof had planned a highly publicized duet between David Bowie and Mick Jagger. The two performers had requested to sing a long-distance duet, with Jagger in Philadelphia and Bowie in London. The technological barriers were considerable, and such a duet would have been marred by time lag. To avoid a potential disaster, both artists arranged a cover version of "Dancing in the Street" by Martha and the Vandellas. The video was premiered at both stadiums and was part of television broadcasts as well.

There were many iconic performances at Live Aid, but one stands out as an historic moment in rock and roll history. In 1985, U2 was a well-known rock band in the United Kingdom, but they were not yet an international phenomenon. At this point, their only American hit was "Pride (In the Name of Love)," which had only reached number thirty-three on the charts. Most viewers knew only that they were from Ireland, so it was logical for Bono to introduce the band with, "We're an Irish band. We come from Dublin City, Ireland." Meanwhile, the English audience was ready to support the band, and U2 flags had been flying throughout the day. The performance begins with "Bad," but after a few minutes, Bono is clearly not satisfied with the audience's lack of response; he drops the microphone and begins pacing the stage, seemingly searching for a more visceral connection or possibly just looking for a memorable moment:

> I don't like the distance between stage and crowd. I don't like the distance between performer and audience, so I'm looking for a symbol of the day. Something I can hold on to. I saw her down there getting crushed, and I thought, "That's it . . ." I didn't know that by holding on to her, I was holding onto the rest of the world. . . . They knew that this kind of wall that they had built up, that we had built up between us and them, was coming down. ("Rockin' All Over")

Bono had seen a young woman who was in the front row, and after a bit of frustrated miming, he jumps down and requests her to be pulled from the audience. The name of the overwhelmed girl is Kal Khalique (she had made it to the front in a quest to see Wham!, not U2), and Bono embraces her, slow dances with her for a few seconds, and kisses her forehead. At this point, he is out of sight of the band, but the stadium video cameras catch this tender moment, and the stadium roars in approval. Bono runs back onstage to finish the set, but time has run short and they cannot perform their biggest hit, "Pride (In the Name of Love)." Larry Mullen, Jr. recalls his frustration: "We were kind of annoyed afterwards because we felt like we'd blown an opportunity to be great. It was our stage, so we felt a little angry about that" ("Rockin' All Over"). Although the members of U2 believed they had lost a unique opportunity, days later they learned that Bono's actions had become one of the most memorable moments of the day. The global exposure that Live Aid provided surely contributed to U2 becoming one of the biggest bands in the world later in the decade.

Sting's new solo career was also influenced by Live Aid. When Geldof initially approached Sting to participate in the program, he immediately ran into the irrepressible Miles Copeland:

> I rang Sting. He was away, but I spoke to Miles Copeland, his manager. 'I'll ask him. Meantime, have you thought about Adam Ant?' I hadn't. I thought he was a bit passé. But then so were the Boomtown Rats, and each represented a certain piece of pop history, so I agreed. I also thought that might entice him to encourage Sting, or perhaps all three of the Police. (Geldof and Vallely, 333)

Unfortunately, no amount of cajoling from Copeland was going to convince Sting to reunite with The Police, and as it turned out, Sting didn't even use a band for Live Aid.

Sting and Phil Collins shared the stage for much of their performance. In addition to the publicity of the Concorde voyage and his smash album, *No Jacket Required*, Collins was approaching the peak of his considerable career in 1985. Sting was only at the start of his solo career; nevertheless, July 1985 was a busy time for him as well. Earlier in the year, he had assembled his new touring band and recorded his crucial first solo album, *The Dream of the Blue Turtles*. In May, the movie *Bring on the Night* was filmed, his first world tour as a solo artist was beginning, and his new son, Jake Sumner, was born. In addition, Sting was becoming more involved in charity movements and had performed his iconic part to "Money for Nothing" with Dire Straits only a couple of weeks before Live Aid at The Prince's Trust Rock Gala, also at Wembley Stadium. Along with his own set, Sting repeated this performance with Dire Straits at Live Aid.

Sting's Live Aid performance was a bit unusual. After he was mistakenly introduced as Phil Collins, he and Branford Marsalis entered the stage wearing all white clothing, looking almost like religious figures. Sting had apparently decided to forgo his touring band to play Wembley Stadium as a duo, a challenging performance combination, regardless of venue. In this duo, Sting played guitar, showing adeptness but not the technical prowess he is capable of on bass, and Marsalis could only provide melodic support. The omission of drums, bass, and keyboards was a risky choice, as the performance could have easily sounded thin and weak, especially in front of 72,000 screaming fans. In his autobiography, Midge Ure asserts that Sting chose the duo format out of defiance because his band had refused to play Live Aid without payment. This may be true but is somewhat unlikely. In July, Sting was largely focused on making media appearances to support his new album. He was not performing much with his group; in fact, they did not perform publicly until August 8 in Tokyo. It is possible that it was simply too much hassle to organize his entire band for a fifteen-minute performance. Furthermore, Sting surely must have known that bands like U2, Queen, and The Who were going to perform riotous sets, so he may have wanted to go in a more subtle direction. Of course, Sting had used this same understated approach during his performance at The

Secret Policeman's Other Ball in 1981, so he was familiar with the versatility and limits of the format.

Ultimately, the risks associated with the duo configuration were overcome by Sting's peerless voice. Viewers were treated to versions of "Roxanne" and "Driven to Tears" that were vocally clear, powerful, and commanding. Sting was eventually joined onstage by Phil Collins, which served to make the set more interesting. Because of his obligations at JFK Stadium, Collins also chose to forgo a band and to only accompany himself on piano, another risky move, as Collins is primarily a drummer, but the strengths of Collins's songs and voice carried the moment.

Although Live Aid was viewed by billions, provided millions of dollars for famine relief, and featured legendary performances, there were still criticisms. Commentators derided the fact that Live Aid did not feature any performances by Africans; they labelled Geldof's goals as short term, mocked the Concorde event as an expensive gimmick, and criticized Geldof for not persuading governments to be more involved. Admittedly, these were valid concerns. But Geldof, who had now taken the role as pop music's conscience, took a more optimistic view of his work:

> The Eighties were characterized by greed. But you must understand, I missed that. For me, the Eighties were characterized by overwhelming generosity and kindness. The period you maybe should be looking at is 1975 to 1985. Maybe that should be "the decade." What Tom Wolfe called the Me Decade in 1977 and what the Boomtown Rats wrote "Looking After No. 1" about in 1976—that selfishness, that greed. Band Aid perhaps signaled the end of that. (Tannenbaum, "Bob Geldof," 80)

Geldof even defended the Concorde "gimmick": "The point was, isn't this amazing? Look what we are capable of doing! And now look at this famine, isn't there something really wrong with this? I mean the whole thing was fraught with symbolism" (Breskin, 33).

A CONSPIRACY OF HOPE AND
HUMAN RIGHTS NOW! TOURS

Much like Geldof's, Sting's career was framed by his activism; only a year after Live Aid, he furthered his involvement with Amnesty International by performing on a short, six-date U.S. tour called A Conspiracy of Hope Tour. Jack Healey, the executive director of Amnesty International USA, who had been instrumental in the success of Amnesty's Secret Policeman's Balls, believed that an all-star tour could raise awareness for Amnesty. The remarkable success of Live Aid surely inspired Healey, but there were marked differences between the two events. First, the goal was to recruit motivated members to Amnesty International, not just to raise funds. During these shows, audience members were asked to not only join Amnesty but to write one letter per month to a government that had denied its citizens human rights—in effect, using the "politics of embarrassment" to convince governments to release unjustly imprisoned citizens. Secondly, unlike Geldof, Healey did not choose artists solely on popularity; instead, his performers had a passion and reputation for activism. Of course, Sting was on the list, but other performers like Peter Gabriel, Bryan Adams, U2, Lou Reed, Joan Baez, and Jackson Browne performed on all six tour dates as well. Lastly, the repertoire of these performers included socially aware tunes, not just their pop hits. While there had been a number of protest songs performed at Live Aid, pop songs like "Caribbean Queen" (Billy Ocean), "Holiday" (Madonna), "Union of the Snake" (Duran Duran), and "Don't Go Breaking My Heart" (Elton John) made up the majority of Live Aid's repertory. Even Sting stuck to a pop repertoire with "Every Breath You Take," certainly his biggest hit but definitely not a protest song. In contrast, the repertoire and production of the A Conspiracy of Hope Tour targeted protest and awareness. For instance, throughout the six shows performers collaborated on particularly important tunes. Bono accompanied Sting during the poignant "Invisible Sun," U2 was usually joined by other performers for "Sun City" (the anti-apartheid song written by Steven Van Zandt), Bob Geldof and Van Zandt performed Bob Marley's "Redemption Song," and the group encore of Bob Dylan's "I Shall be Released" was the highlight of each night. Although there were only six performances, publicity generated by the tour created a growing awareness of Amnesty's work, and performers took considerable pride in what they were accomplishing. Sting considered this tour to be a tool of moral conversion, because he himself had been converted by an Amnesty show:

> I've been a member of Amnesty for five years and a supporter because of an entertainment show which was called The Secret Policeman's Ball, which I was involved in. And before that, I didn't know about Amnesty's work, and so, in a sense, I'm a success story. I know that these kinds of events work. I'm sure that there were 80,000 people there last night; a good proportion of them will want to be supporters and will want to carry on the work. (Gumbel)

The tour began on June 4, 1986, in San Francisco and travelled through Los Angeles, Denver, Atlanta, and Chicago, concluding in New Jersey on June 15. Booking artists of this caliber was a formidable challenge for Healey. June is a busy time in the touring season, and asking world-class artists to not only give up two weeks of revenue but to then perform for free was surely a daunting task. Even Sting acknowledged how difficult it was: "I've been touring for eighteen months and the last thing I want to do is another tour. But I feel Amnesty is so important in what it's trying to achieve, is so utterly important, that everything else is by the board, it doesn't matter" (Gumbel).

The final concert in New Jersey's Giants Stadium lasted from noon to 11 PM. The entire show was telecast on MTV, and the final three hours were aired on the FOX Network. This final show featured an eclectic mix of styles and genres. Artists like Peter, Paul & Mary, Bob Geldof, Stanley Jordan, Joan Armatrading, Howard Jones, Yoko Ono, The Neville Brothers, and Miles Davis performed throughout the day. Later in the evening, when television viewership was at its highest, the biggest acts like U2 were featured. Although Healey had agreed that none of the acts would be paid, the publicity generated by the television broadcasts was payment itself.

When Jack Healey invited Sting to participate in the tour, he also asked if The Police were interested in reuniting. This was a complex request. By June of 1986, Sting had established himself as a solo star, *The Dream of the Blue Turtles* was a hit, and the following world tour was an unqualified success. Furthermore, Sting had experienced artistic freedom in terms of songwriting, arranging, set lists, and so forth. He had also developed a confident, mature, and intelligent persona during interviews and onstage. There was no reason for him to go back to his contentious musical past except to serve Amnesty International and to please Miles Copeland. So Sting agreed to perform the first three shows of the tour with his touring band and the final three shows with The Police, knowing that the reunion would attract even more attention to Amnesty International. Of course, Copeland saw the tour as an excellent opportunity for publicity, and if Sting was impressed by fan demand, maybe he would agree to record with his bandmates again. In the end, Copeland's plan worked. Following the tour, The Police entered the studio with plans to re-record some of their best-known songs, but the combative recording session reminded Copeland, Summers, and Sting that their time as a creative entity was over. The June 15 performance at Giants Stadium was the last time The Police would perform publically until their Rock and Roll Hall of Fame performance in 2003.

Sting's dedication to Amnesty International never wavered, and in 1988 he agreed to participate in a larger version of the A Conspiracy of Hope concerts, called the Human Rights Now! tour. While the former tour focused on American youth, the latter was meant as an international call to join Amnesty International. This time, attendees were urged to become involved with Amnesty by signing the Universal Declaration of Human Rights, and thousands of concertgoers complied. The six-week tour began on September 2, 1988, at Wembley Stadium and moved through Budapest, New Delhi, Harare (Zimbabwe), and Abidjan (Ivory Coast), among other places. Many of these cities were not typical destinations for rock concerts, and even experienced performers like Bruce Springsteen were shocked at the audience's reactions:

> It was a stadium of entirely black faces. Clarence [Clemons] said to me, "Now you know what it feels like!" There were about 60 seconds where you could feel people sussing us out, and then the whole place just exploded. The band came off feeling like it was the first show we'd ever done. We had to go and prove ourselves on just what we were doing that moment on stage. (Greene)

Springsteen, Sting, Tracy Chapman, Peter Gabriel, and Youssou N'Dour headlined the international event and at every stop participated in press conferences emphasizing the importance of universal human rights. Each night's performance aptly concluded with Bob Dylan's "Chimes of Freedom" and Bob Marley's "Get Up, Stand Up."

Jack Healey's productions transformed the image and membership of Amnesty International. When he took over as executive director in 1981, Amnesty had 80,000 members, but after the Human Rights Now! tour there were over 420,000. Healey's concerts also bolstered Sting's persona as an activist, but Sting's most notable activities would be related to his efforts to save portions of the Amazon rain forest.

RAINFOREST FOUNDATION

On November 19, 1987, Sting arrived in Rio de Janeiro to begin a tour of South America that would last through December 12. This was the beginning stage of a tour supporting his newest album, . . . *Nothing Like the Sun*. Sting was very popular in Brazil and throughout South America, so he was booked to perform televised shows for large and enthusiastic audiences in massive stadiums. In some respects, Sting was at the peak of his worldwide popularity. His extraordinary first two solo albums, performances on stages throughout the world, and brilliant appearances on shows like *Saturday Night Live* contributed to an incomparable career. But during these few days in November, Sting's life and career would change forever. Shortly after his arrival in Brazil, Sting learned of the death of his father. Their relationship had been complex and was further complicated by Sting's position as a public figure. Sting had simply not been home enough to work on the fragile relationship. Unfortunately, he wasn't even able to attend his father's funeral because of the publicity it would attract. At this point, Sting might well have been reminded of the limits and privileges of fame. Nonetheless, he performed an intense show at Maracanã Stadium in Rio de Janeiro the following evening. Sting has since admitted that these performances were a form of catharsis, and he was certainly in a retrospective emotional state.

On November 29, the morning after a show at Estádio Mané Garrincha in Brasilia, Sting and his future wife, Trudie Styler, were introduced to the Belgian photographer, filmmaker, and ethnographer Jean-Pierre Dutilleux. Dutilleux and Sting had a connection from the beginning; Dutilleux had directed Stewart Copeland's *The Rhythmatist* in 1985, but more importantly, Dutilleux had spent a considerable amount of time studying the indigenous inhabitants of Brazil. In 1978, he and Luiz Carlos Saldanha codirected the documentary, *Raoni: The Fight for the Amazon*. The Academy Award–nominated film was the product of Dutilleux's interest in the Kayapo tribe since the early 1970s. Dutilleux, who was undoubtedly aware of Sting's charitable interests, convinced him to visit a Kayapo village, which was threatened by logging, mining, road construction, and slash-and-burn agriculture. Sting, Styler, Dutilleux, and percussionist Mino Cinelu immediately flew to the village of Chief Raoni Metuktire. Chief Raoni was a surprisingly charming host who seemed to be aware of Sting's importance. Raoni was no simple-minded tribesman; in 1964 he had met King Leopold III of Belgium and later was the willing subject of Dutilleux's documentary. During the short visit, Sting and Styler were immediately captivated by not only the local battle for Indian rights but also the global impact of deforestation.

Following the trip, Sting and Styler began a campaign to raise awareness for the rain forest's native inhabitants and its slow destruction. When the Human Rights Now! tour reached Sao Paulo, Brazil, in 1988, Sting invited Chief Raoni to participate in the press conference. In February 1989, Sting returned to Brazil and took part in a highly publicized meeting with President José Sarney about the possibility of a Xingu national reserve. In April 1989, Sting and Chief Raoni began a world tour, which included seventeen countries and featured meetings with King Juan Carlos and Queen Sofía of Spain, Francois Mitterrand of France, Bob Hawke of Australia, and even Pope John Paul II.

Also in 1989, Styler and Sting founded the Rainforest Foundation. The purpose of the foundation was to raise awareness and funds by selling merchandise and, of course, organizing benefit concerts. The Rainforest Foundation even published a book, *Jungle Stories*, written by Dutilleux and Sting, to help fund and promote its campaigns. In the book, Sting summarized his position as an activist: "I am not a politician, I am only a singer, but many people listen to me. I promise you that whenever I can speak on your behalf I will do so. I shall tell your story to whomever I can because you are the only protectors of the forest and if the forest dies then so does the earth" (Dutilleux and Sting, 61). In 1993, the foundation successfully lobbied for the first privately funded reserve in the region. Over 17,000 square miles were legally designated for the Kayapo people. Today, the various branches of the Rainforest Foundation work around the world to preserve rain forests. Sting and Styler are no longer actively involved in the day-to-day operations of the foundation, but they still participate in the annual rain forest benefit at Carnegie Hall. To date, this rain forest benefit has raised over $35 million.

Throughout the nineties, Sting's persona was framed by his activist campaigns, and he sometimes suffered for it. Critics complained that he had become too self-righteous and "preachy." Some even pointed to the carbon footprint of Sting's globe-trotting activities, and Sting was compelled to respond, "It's difficult to do my job and not have a carbon footprint, but I've tried to offset it . . . I've worked pretty hard over the past twenty years. I've demarcated an area of land the size of Belgium" (Paxman). Of course, criticism inevitably comes with public campaigns, and ultimately, Sting had no obligation to care about the environment, human rights, or famine. He could easily have bought a Caribbean island and spent his days relaxing; instead, he tried to make a difference. "I think it's naïve to think that a pop star can change the world. All I'm saying is that I have no choice but to make statements. If they have a positive effect, that's great, but I don't expect to change the world. I can only express my feelings" (Harris and Masui).

6

THE POLICE AND THE ROCK TRIO

Since the 1960s, the trio format has held a special, but understudied, place in rock music history. The most prominent formats used throughout much of the modern era of rock have been quartets (bass, drums, guitar, and vocalist) and quintets (bass, drums, guitar, vocalist, and a keyboard instrument or second guitarist). The number of widely popular and influential rock trios is remarkably small, but this scarcity is not apparent in other types of music. For instance, jazz history boasts many acclaimed trios; the piano trios of Keith Jarrett, Bill Evans, and Brad Melhdau are regarded as some of the most influential jazz groups of all time. Also in the jazz realm, organ trios led by George Benson, Jimmy Smith, and Medeski Martin & Wood have earned praise from the jazz community for decades. In country music, trios like Lady Antebellum, Dixie Chicks, and Rascal Flatts have reached the highest levels of popularity and acclaim. Western art music also includes a rich history of string, brass, and woodwind trios, which can be traced back for centuries. However, in rock history, comparatively few trios have reached the highest levels of historical popularity and influence while exclusively performing as a "true trio."

This is not to say that successful rock trios don't exist. Groups like Alkaline Trio, Dinosaur Jr., The Jam, Motörhead, Primus, Sleater-Kinney, and The Stray Cats are just a few of the hundreds of prominent rock trios. Nevertheless, as creative and entertaining as these bands may be, they are not historically regarded as exceptionally popular. Many rock purists may scoff at the notion of popularity, but few can argue with the fact that mainstream acceptance leads to a broader scope of influence. How does one gauge the historical popularity and influence of any given rock trio? One easy way is to ask: could the group support an international, arena-based tour during any time of its existence? If the answer is "yes," then that rock trio is part of a remarkably short list.

One important benchmark for the list of elite rock trios can be determined by performance practice. Simply put, did the trio regularly perform as a trio, or did they typically include supporting members? This is an important question, because performing as a trio is a profoundly different experience than performing as a larger group. While the addition of a fourth or fifth band member may seem to have a negligible effect on performing, this is not the case. The typical rock trio format of bass, drums, and guitar, with one instrumentalist also singing, places the responsibility of the essential elements of performance, harmony, melody, and rhythm squarely on the shoulders of each member. Each performer must be competent enough to handle his or her part without help. There may be no keyboardist to fill out harmonies, rhythm guitarist to accompany solos, or dedicated singer. There is nowhere to "hide" as a member of a trio. You must perform your part, or the group will fail. Furthermore, the trio format frequently requires that musicians perform more than one part. For example, performers like Sting and Geddy Lee have mastered the art of singing while simultaneously playing intricate bass lines. As a guitarist, Andy Summers learned to be an excellent soloist as well as a colorful accompanist. Although drummers are rarely asked to perform more than one instrument at a time, they are sometimes tasked with singing background vocal parts and creating drum patterns that contribute character and energy to the group. In fact, some of the most respected drummers in rock history, like Stewart Copeland, Neil Peart, Ginger Baker, and Mitch Mitchell, have been members of rock trios. Lastly, the trio format requires a considerable amount of concentration and creative energy during performances. In large venues, groups like Rush, Green Day, and The Police are tasked with producing a remarkably high level of power through virtuosity and concentration. Once again, as a trio there is nowhere to hide, so the responsibility of entertaining thousands of fans is placed on only three artists.

Keeping these criteria in mind, Cream, The Jimi Hendrix Experience, Rush, The Police, Nirvana, and Green Day are members of a short list of elite popular and influential rock trios. Moreover, they are exemplars and pre-eminent representatives of their respective genres. What bands provide better mainstream representations of psychedelic rock, progressive rock, new wave, grunge, and punk than these trios? Though there are a few other fine rock trios with substantial fan bases who could arguably be a part of the list, like Emerson, Lake & Palmer, Blink 182, and Muse, they regrettably take a secondary historical role when compared to their more long-lived peers like Rush and Green Day. And as will be seen, The Police have a variety of personal and historical relationships with each of these groups.

CREAM

Cream set the standard by which most other rock trios are measured. The power, creativity, and virtuosity of Jack Bruce, Eric Clapton, and Ginger Baker embodied what a rock trio could achieve. In many regards, Cream is the first rock trio to reach mainstream success, yet their repertoire was an eclectic mix of typical 1960s-era rock songs, such as "Sunshine of Your Love" and "White Room," with more psychedelic and improvisational tunes, such as "Spoonful" and "Tales of Brave Ulysses." During live performances, these songs were the basis for extended improvisations, which reflected the boundless creativity of the 1960s rock scene. Although many have attempted to define what Cream was, Clapton may have summarized it best: "People wanted to hear us just jam, so we gave them that. That's what the group was really all about. A sort of rolling jam session with songs as excuses" (Clapton). Ultimately, this rolling jam session was the result of the musical personalities brought to the band by each member.

Prior to forming Cream, Eric Clapton had played with The Roosters and Casey Jones and the Engineers, and in October 1963, he joined The Yardbirds. Even at this early stage of his career, he was primarily interested in combining the urban blues stylings inspired by guitarists like B. B. King and Buddy Guy with the burgeoning London rock-and-roll scene. Initially, the Yardbirds' repertoire featured a variety of covers of American blues artists such as Bo Diddley, Howlin' Wolf, Sonny

Boy Williamson, Willie Dixon, and Chuck Berry. By 1965, the extraordinary popularity of The Beatles prompted The Yardbirds to integrate more pop influences into their repertoire, resulting in their first hit, "For Your Love." Coincidently, "For Your Love" was written by Graham Gouldman, a future member of 10cc, whose bandmates Kevin Godley and Lol Creme would later direct videos for The Police and Sting. Even with the success of "For Your Love," Clapton was no longer satisfied with the musical direction of The Yardbirds and recommended Jimmy Page as his replacement. Page deferred, but another future guitar virtuoso, Jeff Beck, happily replaced Clapton. Seeking a more blues-centric musical environment, Clapton joined John Mayall and the Blues Breakers in April 1965. While with Mayall, Clapton solidified his reputation as a formidable blues guitarist—so much so that the graffiti tag "Clapton is God" began appearing throughout London's subway stations during the mid-1960s. In November, a gifted young drummer named Ginger Baker sat in with Mayall's group, and Clapton was impressed.

Following a recommendation by Charlie Watts, Ginger Baker joined Blues Incorporated in 1962. This group was an important part of London's burgeoning blues scene and employed a variety of other musicians, including Jack Bruce. Baker, nicknamed "Ginger" because of his red hair, helped form The Graham Bond Organisation in 1963 with a few of his former bandmates from Blues Incorporated, bassist Jack Bruce, organist Graham Bond, and saxophonist Dick Heckstall-Smith. Baker encouraged The Graham Bond Organisation to incorporate a high level of musicianship within their R&B, jazz, and blues repertoire. Although The Graham Bond Organisation achieved little commercial success, it was representative of a more serious kind of pop music, which influenced a variety of young musicians. One of these musicians, Sting, included his impressions of this era in his autobiography.

> When I am fifteen years old, the first live band I ever see is there: the Graham Bond Organisation. . . . The music is harsh and uncompromising and I'm not sure if I like it, but I have a strong sense that what is being played has a weight and seriousness that will later be characterized and then caricatured as "heavy." (*Broken Music*, 82)

Baker's "heaviness" was steeped in a tradition created by jazz drummers like Max Roach, Art Blakey, and Elvin Jones. This tradition favored an advanced rhythmic approach and skill set, featuring syncopation, polyrhythms, and an intuitive time feel. Baker was certainly not your typical blues/rock drummer, and he quickly grew bored with Graham Bond's musical direction. Much like Clapton, Baker was looking for a new musical challenge.

Meanwhile, bassist Jack Bruce was also looking for new musical directions. Bruce had prior professional relationships with Baker and Clapton. He had been bandmates with Baker in Blues Incorporated and The Graham Bond Organisation, but by August 1965, they were at odds. Mutual attempts at sabotage and even physical threats by Baker led to Bruce's firing from The Graham Bond Organisation. Bruce soon joined John Mayall and the Blues Breakers, and of course, Eric Clapton was the guitarist. One reason for Bruce's seemingly easy transition from one excellent band to another was his unquestionable talent and versatility. Much like Baker, Bruce's musical background was grounded in jazz. His father introduced him to jazz greats like Louis Armstrong and Fats Waller, and by the early 1960s he was in demand as a bassist and vocalist in London's blues scene. In 1966, Bruce once again moved on to another band, Manfred Mann. During March 1966, he rejoined Clapton in Powerhouse. This short-lived band, which included Steve Winwood on vocals, was put together for an Elektra Records compilation album featuring English talent. Although only three tracks were recorded, two of the three, "Steppin' Out" and "Crossroads," would become part of Cream's repertoire.

During a drive home in the summer of 1966, Ginger Baker gauged Clapton's interest in forming a new rock trio. Clapton was immediately receptive to the idea: "I had seen Buddy Guy play at the Marquee with a trio, so I had it in my mind that the trio was the ideal combo size" ("Classic Albums"). Baker's excitement was quickly cut short when Clapton requested that Jack Bruce play bass. Baker had no choice but to accept, knowing that he might have difficulty reconciling with Bruce. On July 29, 1966, Cream unofficially debuted at the Twisted Wheel nightclub in Manchester, and a few days later, they publicly debuted at the Windsor Jazz & Blues Festival.

Cream recorded four albums, *Fresh Cream* (1966), *Disraeli Gears* (1967), *Wheels of Fire* (1968), and *Goodbye* (1969), which were accompanied by heavy performing and recording schedules. The hectic touring, drug use, ear-splitting volumes, and continual hostility between

Baker and Bruce inevitably led Cream to unofficially disband by mid-1968, although the band continued to tour and record under duress until November of that year. They reunited for their 1993 induction into the Rock and Rock Hall of Fame and again for a short series of concerts in 2005. Sadly, when Jack Bruce died in 2014, any possibility of another Cream reunion died along with him.

Despite the brevity of their tenure, Cream was extraordinarily influential. As individuals, they displayed an instrumental bravura that appealed to thousands of young musicians. For instance, Stewart Copeland was particularly drawn to Ginger Baker's powerful and commanding drum style: "I must have been sixteen. It must have been the sweet spot where my brain clicked on and said, 'What's it all about.' It was Ginger's drums" (*Beware of Mr. Baker*). Baker and Copeland held similar positions in their respective bands. In Baker's case, Clapton and Bruce certainly contributed the content and structure to many of their songs, but Baker provided the wild energy that defined so many of their live performances. The same can be said for Copeland's role with The Police. Sting and Summers undoubtedly provided the majority of the lyrical and melodic content, but during live performances Copeland's vitality and inventiveness helped make The Police so unique.

Andy Summers inadvertently played an important role in the history of Cream. In the mid-1960s, Summers purchased a 1959 Les Paul Sunburst model from a small music store in central London. Eric Clapton, a musical colleague of Summers, asked him where he had purchased it and promptly bought one for himself. Unfortunately, Clapton's guitar was stolen in early 1966, and he asked Summers if he would sell his own Les Paul. After some thought, Summers agreed to sell his guitar to Clapton, and rock history was made:

> The next day I drop off the Les Paul at Advision in the West End, where Eric's in the middle of recording with Jack and Ginger. Not wanting to hang around, I hand the guitar over to the kid at the front desk and tell him to give it to Clapton. I go into the toilet at the side of the reception area and when I come out I can hear Eric's voice over the PA system, which is inadvertently hooked into the foyer. He is remarking how great the guitar is, just like his old one. I feel a rush of seller's remorse and get the Green Line back to West Kensington with "I'm So Glad" rolling through my head.

Eric records *Fresh Cream* with my Les Paul, becomes a guitar hero, is identified with this guitar—the terms *Les Paul* and *Clapton* become synonymous—the star of the '59 Sunburst begins to ascend. Before Clapton it was regarded as a weird failure, but after *Fresh Cream* the little Gibson becomes the absolute guitar. What if I hadn't sold my guitar to Eric? Maybe it would all have turned out differently, and the Les Paul would have been merely another interesting historical clunker rather than a cultural icon. But possibly because of our little interchange, it becomes a Stradivarius of rock guitars. (*One Train Later*, 71)

Cream set the standard for what a trio could accomplish in pop music. The band's international fame relied on recordings that demonstrated a unique combination of instrumental virtuosity, psychedelic lyrics and imagery, and raw power. But beyond the recordings, Cream was regarded as an extraordinary live band. Onstage, the group created an environment of exploration; neither the audience nor the band members knew where each song was going to end up. Concertgoers did not dance or even communicate with each other very much. Cream was a "listening music." Admittedly, you *had* to listen because the group could be extraordinarily loud, but Bruce's operatic voice, Clapton's blues accents, and Baker's relentless rhythms created a churning machine of creativity with limitless possibilities that were impossible to ignore. This kind of improvisationally based popular music faded quickly from the mainstream; later rock trios like Rush, The Police, and Nirvana would depend more on songwriting than on open-ended musical explorations, but not before another improvisational trio would take rock music by storm.

THE JIMI HENDRIX EXPERIENCE

Ironically, the tenures of two of the most influential rock trios in rock history, Cream and The Jimi Hendrix Experience, occurred almost simultaneously. Cream expanded the parameters of what a power trio could be: endlessly creative, spontaneous, and intuitive. But most importantly, their individual musical personalities were compelling enough to capture the attention of millions of listeners. In other words, Cream was a team effort. On the other hand, The Jimi Hendrix Experience inarguably centered on the virtuosity of Jimi Hendrix, who not only epitomized the virtuoso guitarist, but embodied the visual and musical aesthetics of rock music at the end of the 1960s.

The circumstances of Hendrix's tragic death are well known, but he had an equally tragic childhood. He was born on November 27, 1942, at Seattle's King County Hospital. His parents, Al and Lucille Hendrix, battled alcohol issues throughout much of his childhood. They divorced when he was nine years old, with Al gaining custody of Hendrix and his siblings. In 1958, Lucille died from complications of alcohol use; Hendrix also got his first guitar. He enlisted in the U.S. Army in 1961 and was assigned to the 101st Airborne Division, but was discharged in 1962. There is some conjecture over why Hendrix was discharged, but his platoon sergeant, James C. Spears, wrote in 1962 that Hendrix was simply not a good soldier: "He has no interest whatsoever in the Army. . . . It is my opinion that Private Hendrix will never come up to the standards required of a soldier. I feel that the military service will benefit if he is discharged as soon as possible" (Roby and Schreiber, 24).

By the mid-1960s Hendrix was working as a sideman for a variety of well-known artists like Sam Cooke, Jackie Wilson, Little Richard, and the Isley Brothers. In 1966 he moved to Greenwich Village, New York, and led his own group, Jimmy James and the Blue Flames. It was during a performance with the Blue Flames that Linda Keith, Keith Richards's girlfriend, met Hendrix and referred him to Chas Chandler. Chandler, coincidentally born in the same town as Sting, was resigning as bassist for The Animals when he met Hendrix in 1966. Chandler convinced Hendrix that English audiences were ready for another guitar god, and Hendrix promptly moved to London in September. Chandler quickly organized auditions for a bassist and drummer.

Hendrix reportedly chose bassist Noel Redding because of his interest in rhythm and blues and his wild hairstyle. Up to this point, Redding had mostly performed on guitar but switched to bass in order to perform with Hendrix. Admittedly, Hendrix could have found a more gifted bassist—many were certainly available in 1966—but at this point Hendrix clearly prized a stylish personality over musical prowess. Mitch Mitchell, on the other hand, was a perfect fit for the new rock trio. By the mid-1960s, Mitchell had performed with The Pretty Things, The Riot Squad, and Georgie Fame and the Blue Flames, earning a reputation as a fine touring and recording musician. When Georgie Fame and the Blue Flames disbanded in October 1966, Mitchell was immediately contacted by Chandler to audition for the new trio. After the audition, only Mitchell and Aynsley Dunbar were left, so Hendrix and Chandler reportedly tossed a coin to determine who the drummer would be. Much like Ginger Baker, Mitchell's background was indebted to jazz drummers like Elvin Jones and Art Blakey. Mitchell not only provided a dense rhythmic foundation for Hendrix's extended improvisations, but he also incorporated a powerful undercurrent of polyrhythm into the group's sound.

The Jimi Hendrix Experience embodied nearly every compelling aspect of rock in the late 1960s. Redding's pulsing bass lines laid down a foundation for Mitchell's churning rhythms, both of which provided Hendrix with a responsive accompaniment that enabled him to explore limitless musical territories. Moreover, the bandmates wore outlandishly colorful clothing that visually reflected the psychedelic era. When Sting watched *Top of the Pops* in December 1966, featuring Hendrix, he was overcome by the entire experience:

> Hendrix had transformed "Hey Joe," an old folk song, and propelled it by the elegant ferocity of his guitar playing into a sassy, bluesy vehicle of awesome power. His vocal was as sulky and offhand as it was passionate and openly sexual, and as the three-piece band stormed through the three-minute song, I imagined everyone in whole the country in front of their tellys sitting bolt upright in their chairs. *Wow! What the fuck was that?*" (*Broken Music*, 83)

In March 1967, the teenaged Sting boldly attended a live performance by Hendrix at a local Newcastle club called Club A' Go Go. The performers were obligated to perform both an early and late show, and during the early show, Hendrix pushed his guitar through the ceiling plasterboard while continuing to play. Hendrix had performed this stunt before and knew of its potential impact on the audience. The stunt worked, and a young Sting would never be the same:

> The Jimi Hendrix Experience was an overwhelming, deafening wave of sound that simply obliterated analysis. I think I remember snatches of "Hey Joe" and "Foxy Lady," but that event remains a blur of noise and breathtaking virtuosity, of Afro'd hair, wild clothes, and

towers of Marshall amplifiers. It was also the first time I'd ever seen
a black man. I remember Hendrix creating a hole in the plaster
ceiling above the stage with the head of his guitar, and then it was
over. I lay in my bed that night with my ears ringing and my world-
view significantly altered. (*Broken Music*, 85)

The music performed that day clearly had an impact on Sting, but he
gives equal emphasis to the overall look and sound of the show as well.
The wild clothes and Afro'd hair were a vital component of the concert,
and many others would surely agree. Sting cites the volume of the band
as being remarkable as well. Mitch Mitchell was responsible for intro-
ducing Hendrix to the power of amplification. During a performance at
Ronnie Scott's, Hendrix had tried a Marshall amplifier for the first time
and was impressed. Coincidentally, Jim Marshall, who owned a music
store in west London, had given Mitch Mitchell a series of drum lessons, and they had developed a close relationship. Mitchell introduced
Hendrix to Marshall:

So, Mitch brought him along to my shop, and this tall, lanky
American said to me, "I'm going to be the greatest, man." I thought,
"Christ, another American wants something for nothing!" And yet a
few breaths later he said, "Now, I don't want to be given anything—I
want to pay the full retail price" . . . Jimi bought three stacks. (Maloof, 59)

New technology had a sizable impact on the band's overall aesthetic.
Redding performed on an array of electric basses with the requisite wall
of Sunn amplifiers, while Hendrix took advantage of the increasing
availability of electronics by utilizing innovative guitar effects like the
wah-wah pedal, Octavia, and the Uni-Vibe.

Sting, and most of the world, may have experienced The Jimi Hendrix Experience from a distance, but Andy Summers, who was the same
age as Hendrix, actually performed with him. On October 27, 1968,
Summers happened to be at TTG Studios in Hollywood, California,
during a Hendrix recording session. Remarkably, Summers summoned
the courage to begin an impromptu jam session with Hendrix during a
break:

I pick up a guitar that's lying there and start jamming along with
Mitch. A few minutes later Jimi comes back out into the studio and

picks up a bass and starts jamming along with us. *Christ*, I think, in a hallucinatory flash, *Jimi Hendrix is playing bass with me.* But I don't freak out or stop but just carry on playing. This might be (a) the greatest act of self-confidence of all time, (b) incredible arrogance, (c) my being medicated to the eyeballs, or (d) deafness, but we continue for about ten minutes and then Jimi says, "Hey, man, do you mind if I play guitar for a while?" "Sure," I say, trying to be cool as if this is an everyday occurrence—all musicians are in total awe of Hendrix at this point and I fight against breaking down into a sobbing heap. (*One Train Later*, 124)

In the cases of Sting and Summers, the power and vitality of Hendrix's band left an indelible impression that influenced the music of both musicians.

RUSH

Although the members of Rush admit to being influenced by other rock trios like Cream, Jimi Hendrix, and The Police, they have created their own distinctive musical legacy. Few bands have been as long lived, and even fewer have created a repertoire that spans so many diverse musical genres. During various points of its existence, Rush has performed a repertoire influenced by hard rock, progressive rock, new wave, reggae, western art music, and countless others. Rush did not represent these genres only in the occasional song; rather, they created multiple albums utilizing and codifying the most relevant characteristics of these genres. Nevertheless, the genre Rush most thoroughly embraced and ultimately embodied is progressive rock.

Of the many compelling aspects of Rush, the relationship between bassist/vocalist Geddy Lee and guitarist Alex Lifeson is arguably the most interesting. The two performers have remained close for over forty-five years. In 1967, the two were schoolmates at Fisherville Junior High in a suburb of Toronto. "We came from pretty much the same neighborhood. We met in the eighth grade. Alex used to borrow my amplifier all the time. We played in coffee shops for chips and gravy. I worked in my mother's hardware store for a while. Alex worked in a gas station" (Swenson). When the boys decided to form a band in 1968, they looked to the blues-inspired rock bands of the late 1960s: "We were playing the English blues—John Mayall, Cream. Alex would pretend he was Eric Clapton, I would pretend I was Jack Bruce, and we'd play 'Spoonful' for twenty minutes" (Swenson). Along with drummer John Rutsey, the trio embarked on the long road to success by performing for unresponsive audiences in unaccommodating venues. During these difficult early years, the group's experimentations with progressive rock alienated some listeners, resulting in Rush's record company demanding a more mainstream approach. Nevertheless, after the inclusion of drummer Neil Peart in 1974, who would become the band's primary lyricist, Rush became even more ensconced in the progressive rock aesthetic throughout the 1970s. The group's repertoire embodied the most revered elements of progressive rock: odd meters, eccentric lyrics, and complex song forms.

By 1980, Rush began to move away from the overt complexities of progressive rock and towards a shorter, catchier, and more radio-friendly repertoire. The band had always been willing to draw on the music of the day, and new wave was one of the most compelling styles available. Neil Peart admits,

> I was a huge fan of The Police and Ultravox and all these new English bands. I loved them. It became a part of our sensibility. *Permanent Waves* still had a number of longer songs on it, but "The Spirit of Radio" was the emblematic song of that period. The mix of sounds in it. The approach to electronic music and reggae, that's all the stuff I was listening to. (*Rush: Beyond the Lighted Stage*)

Memorable pop songs like "Tom Sawyer," "Limelight," and "The Spirit of Radio" made Rush an extraordinarily popular mainstream touring act, but the band's die-hard fans missed the more virtuosic and daring compositions of the 1970s. In the 1990s, these fans were pleased to hear Rush return to progressive rock by incorporating more emphasis on Lifeson's guitar and less on electronic keyboards. Even after a hiatus prompted by the tragic deaths of Peart's daughter and wife in the late 1990s, the band reunited in 2001 and continues to produce musically compelling albums.

Rush has remained a viable creative entity largely because of the remarkable friendship between Geddy Lee and Alex Lifeson. The stress of recording, promotion, and touring over the course of decades can weaken even the strongest relationships. Popular music history is strewn with bands that achieved the highest levels of success, only to break up soon after. In fact, disbanding after sudden success is one of the most common narratives in pop music. Yet Rush perseveres. Lifeson is certainly aware of this unique relationship, "There are very, very few bands that get along anything like as well as we do. In fact, thinking about all the bands I've ever met, I really don't think there are any" (Fitzpatrick). On stage, Geddy and Lifeson combine friendly banter with amazing musicianship, but they are frequently seen together off stage as well. Somehow they have kept their relationship playful and fresh. Admittedly, Peart has been known to be a bit introverted, but it is clear that his bandmates have developed a relationship of understanding and mutual respect with him as well.

Of course, the longevity of Rush cannot be attributed to the band alone. Rush has an unusually dedicated fan base. Considering the radical stylistic changes that Rush has undergone during the last forty years, it is remarkable that they have attracted fans who pride themselves on knowing the smallest detail of Rush's considerable repertoire. A Rush concert features mostly white male listeners, miming the slightest musical movement. These audiences are proud of their loyalty, their detailed knowledge of every aspect of the group, their determination to never leave concerts early, and, most importantly, they are proud of being part of arguably the nerdiest fan base in pop music. In some ways, Rush's devotees are outsiders. Many in the popular music community have never embraced Rush—the band was not inducted into the Rock and Roll Hall of Fame until 2013—and Rush's fans feel that they are a part of this marginalization as well. As Alex Lifeson states, there is a unique bond between Rush and their fans: "There is a segment of our audience that are outsiders and some have grown into power and influence, but that bond they feel to us is still there. It's very, very deep and I don't think it's like that for a lot of other bands" (Fitzpatrick).

A contributing factor to the marginalization of Rush and its fans is the band's reliance on virtuosity and the resultant "cult of virtuosity" that surrounds them. Rush's repertoire incorporates shifting meters, odd phrasing, technically demanding musical passages, and highly sophisticated drum patterns, and they somehow replicate these elements during live performances. Their shows are regarded as technical spectacles that not only entertain but amaze those who are privy to the mastery that is taking place onstage. The devotees of Rush are sometimes obsessed with the gear, practice routines, technical exercises, and even the postures of each musician. There are chatrooms, online forums, conventions, and magazines that feature and venerate Lee, Peart, and Lifeson. Within this community, the three are treated as instrumental gods. Even some well-known musicians like Kirk Hammett and Billy Corgan admit to being part of this cult of virtuosity; says Hammet, "I looked at the album cover and saw that there were only three of them. And they were wearing some funky clothes, but I thought, 'How can three guys make such a sound.'" Corgan states, "I knew how to play *2112* all the way down. I knew every note, every moment. I think back now and think, 'how did I fucking learn that?' I must have sat in the bedroom for a year to learn that fucking song" (*Rush: Beyond*). Some critics, and even other groups like The Police, criticized Rush's use of virtuosity by labeling them as "old-fashioned prog rockers." An ironic criticism, because The Police have their own cult of virtuosity. In fact, the trio format inherently demands a high level of musicianship.

The nature of the rock trio requires that the vocalist also perform an instrument. In the case of Rush and The Police, the lead singer also plays bass. Admittedly, pop music features many vocalists who simultaneously play an instrument, but it is usually a guitar. A bass playing vocalist is more rare, and for good reason. A guitar may be strummed using motions that can be repetitive and relatively easy to master, thus allowing the singer to focus on singing and communicating with the crowd. The bass, on the other hand, is the harmonic and rhythmic foundation of any band, and its nature is to create a counterpoint to the melody. In other words, the vocalist/bassist usually performs two distinct melodies at the same time. Sting describes the difficulty of learning to sing and play bass simultaneously:

> Playing the bass and singing is not as natural as strumming on a guitar and singing. There is a certain amount of neural and muscular independence required, something like riding a bike and juggling at the same time. While I certainly put in the required hours trying to perfect this combination of skills, I also begin to rationalize the bass parts so that I have more freedom to sing, leaving gaps that I would normally have filled. In doing this, I begin to develop the genesis of a style, a spare and economic bass signature that I would later justify as part of a deliberate "less is more" ethos, but it really comes out of the

necessity of having to deal with my own limitations. (*Broken Music*, 163)

Indeed, Geddy Lee and Sting share in performing the uppermost melody and the foundational bass line simultaneously, a considerable task.

Stewart Copeland and Neil Peart are mutually surrounded by a cult of virtuosity as well. Specialist magazines like *Modern Drummer* have featured both drummers countless times, and they are the subject of endless debates over "who's the best drummer in history." Even David Letterman, a member of the drummer cult of virtuosity, invited each performer for his "drum solo week" series. Yet Peart and Copeland have attracted this adoration in markedly different ways. Peart's drumming is a model of technical brilliance. Behind an enormous drum set, he powers through multi-metered passages with a combination of grace, brute power, and technical showmanship. Copeland, on the other hand, displays a sense of spontaneity, creativity, and energy that is difficult to define and impossible to replicate.

Rush's legacy can be framed by their musical prowess, genre shifts, fan base, and longevity, but they are also a part of a larger history of rock trios. Rush, possibly above all others, demonstrates what a trio can accomplish in a live setting, and they arguably set the standard by which progressive rock is judged. Another trio, Nirvana, defined grunge in an even more potent fashion.

NIRVANA

In the early 1990s, grunge bands such as Pearl Jam, Soundgarden, Alice in Chains, and Stone Temple Pilots were enjoying an unprecedented level of notoriety. They were part of an immense surge of interest in the grunge aesthetic. This aesthetic included fashion, hairstyles, and attitudes. Grunge had become a generational signpost for young people around the world. But no other band, personality, or fashion statement defined grunge more than the rock trio Nirvana. This band captured the attention of millions of listeners, who made Nirvana one of the biggest bands in the world virtually overnight. Nirvana's success was a surprise to most in the recording industry and even to the band itself. During the release of its breakout album, *Nevermind*, Nirvana was participating in an extended European tour supporting another alternative band, Sonic Youth. Because of this inopportune scheduling, the band didn't experience the initial explosion of interest that followed the release of *Nevermind*. In fact, mainstream success was never a goal; as Dave Grohl notes, "We had that do it yourself, punk rock ethic that we all shared. I don't think it would have worked if one didn't have that. Honestly, there was hardly any career ambition at all. We knew that there was no way we could be the biggest band in the world. We just wanted to play" (*VH1 Classic Albums*). Nevertheless, Nirvana ended up being the leading proponent of grunge and has since held a prominent historical position, for better or worse, as the exemplar of the genre.

The grunge movement is historically tied to the Seattle area music community, of which Kurt Cobain and Krist Novoselic were a part in the late 1980s. Cobain and Novoselic had developed a relationship through a common interest in rock bands like Black Sabbath, Black Flag, Van Halen, The Beatles, and a local band, Melvins. In fact, Melvins lead singer Buzz Osborne is an unlikely hero of rock history. It was he who took Cobain to his first hard-core rock show, which featured the band Black Flag, and Osborne ultimately introduced drummer Dave Grohl to Cobain and Novoselic as well. With the addition of Grohl in late 1990, Nirvana forged a sound that incorporated Cobain's introspective lyrics and intuitive sense of melody with the distortion of heavy metal and chaos of punk. Butch Vig brilliantly recorded and produced this distinctive sound in 1991 for the album *Nevermind*. The bold sound of the album was even more remarkable in light of the fact that Nirvana was only a trio; according to Grohl,

> Playing drums with Nirvana was a process of simplification. I didn't want to be the guy from Rush, who's awesome, he's an amazing drummer, but we tried to pack as much into four minutes with just these three simple elements. It really was a powerful group in that each sound was just huge because there was nothing in the way. (Stewart)

Indeed, the inherent directness of the trio format may have contributed to the powerful sound that Nirvana created.

Although another Seattle-based band, Pearl Jam, had achieved some recognition by 1991, the overwhelming popularity of *Nevermind* made Nirvana the de facto face of grunge and the entire Seattle music scene.

Nevermind's popularity was due to a variety of reasons. First, Kurt Cobain was a charismatic lead singer. His blonde good looks hid a dark personality that was irresistible to many female fans. Furthermore, the imaginative and sinister video for "Smells Like Teen Spirit" was placed on heavy rotation on MTV, ensuring maximum exposure for the band. In addition, the trio's wild antics and anti-establishment stance were particularly attractive to an audience that was searching for an "authentic" band to echo their own sense of alienation and angst. Lastly, *Nevermind* featured a gritty and harsh sound unlike any of its contemporaries. In late 1991 and 1992, slickly produced mainstream artists like Michael Jackson, Garth Brooks, Billy Ray Cyrus, and Kriss Kross dominated the *Billboard* charts. For young rock fans, the rawness of *Nevermind* was a bright beacon of hope. Today, Nirvana is presented as the exemplar of 1990s grunge music in every popular music history textbook, and "Smells Like Teen Spirit" is a typical subject for musical analysis in many of these texts.

Nevermind introduced the world to Seattle as well as to the grunge aesthetic. Young people began wearing flannel and Doc Marten boots, growing their hair out, and publically proclaiming their distrust for corporations and government. But by the mid-1990s, grunge was only one element of the systematic mainstreaming of Seattle. Companies like Starbucks and Microsoft had made Seattle the capital of corporate innovation, while films like *Singles* and *Sleepless in Seattle* set the city as a symbol of liberalism and youth. Unfortunately, this newfound attention to the city and its most famous export, grunge, created generic labels that stripped the individuality away from the bands that made up the Seattle music community. Of course, the inherent limits of genre labels like grunge are also apparent in other genres such as new wave, the label assigned to The Police a decade earlier.

At first glance, new wave and grunge have little in common. One is synonymous with the stylized and synthesizer-driven music of the 1980s, and the other recalls the turgid and angst-filled rock of the 1990s. Yet both labels are problematic, for similar reasons. Most definitions of new wave include bands like The Police, Devo, The Cars, Talking Heads, Duran Duran, and Elvis Costello. How valid or meaningful is a label that includes such diverse artists? Surprisingly, little has been written on the categorizing of new wave. Scholar Theo Cateforis believes that the term was initially a signifier of difference between the traditions of rock and the modernity of the new wave in the early 1980s, but the term was quickly co-opted as a catch-all classifying label that eventually lost all real meaning. Artists like Sting have resisted the media's obsessive use of generic labels, because some music defies definition. The same can be said for the term grunge. Nirvana may have been the face of grunge, but other groups like Pearl Jam, Mudhoney, Tad, Soundgarden, Alice in Chains, Stone Temple Pilots, and Screaming Trees were also placed under the grunge umbrella. These groups had little in common, but the marketing power of the term grunge was so great in the early 1990s that companies used it to define almost any group that incorporated distortion or angst-driven lyrics in their music. Much like Sting, many of these Seattle-based musicians shunned any labeling.

In the end, Cobain's discomfort with popularity and the stress of being the leader of such a popular band and social movement led to significant personal issues. Nevertheless, Nirvana's punk-inspired skepticism still exists in today's youth, and Novoselic is rightfully proud of Nirvana's anti-establishment legacy: "There's one thing you have to remember about Nirvana. Nirvana didn't go to the mainstream, the mainstream came to Nirvana" (*VH1 News Special*). The mainstream would also be a point of contention with another popular trio of the 1990s.

GREEN DAY

Green Day currently tours and records with additional musicians, but for much of their early history they performed as a trio. As with the other trios mentioned, Green Day performs with a relentless energy that belies the fact that there are only three musicians on stage. Although Billie Joe Armstrong, Mike Dirnt, and Tré Cool have been touring together since the early 1990s, their live performances are a procession of hard-charging punk and rock tunes that offer little respite for their enthusiastic audiences. The band's combination of pop sensibility, punk ambivalence, and rock vitality has made them one of the best-selling bands in pop history. Much like The Police, their worldwide success originated within marginalized punk communities, who ultimately rejected them. Nevertheless, Green Day's punk origins and personal experiences contributed to a lyrical depth that led to unlikely success. In the end, Green Day's distinctive musical and performing aesthetic helped set the paradigm for punk music's revival in the 1990s and again in the 2000s.

Billie Joe Armstrong and Mike Dirnt met at the age of ten while attending Carquinez Middle School in Rodeo, California. Armstrong and Dirnt bonded through a mutual interest in music, and both young men were undergoing significant personal issues. Armstrong's father had recently died of cancer, and his mother was working as a waitress. Dirnt had been put up for adoption as an infant and later endured the divorce of his adoptive parents. These experiences forged a remarkable bond between the two young men, who were looking toward music for self-identification and stability. They found kinship within the California punk community, more specifically, at an alternative music venue named 924 Gilman Street, located in Berkeley, California.

By the late 1980s, fans of punk music were a marginalized community. Mainstream rock music was comprised of colorful but vapid bands like Poison, Mötley Crüe, Ratt, and Skid Row. Punk audiences were pushed into small venues like Gilman Street and thus formed closely knit communities. Armstrong saw Gilman Street as almost a second family:

> I had a place called Gilman Street, it was a punk-rock club up in Berkeley, and I was just introduced to a lot of new ideas. I think that was my escape. And there was another moment in time where I felt empowered because I was getting another education that I wasn't getting at home anymore, or from the schools that I had to go to. It was just this feeling of, "I'm out of prison." (Gross)

These young fans, like Armstrong, shared a love for the same high-tempo beats and defiant lyrics that attracted audiences in the late 1970s. In fact, Green Day's early performances at Gilman are remarkably similar to early performances of The Police in London punk clubs. The songs are short, aggressive, energetic, and fueled by youthful energy. Unlike most punk bands of both eras, though, The Police and Green Day had melodic sensibilities and instrumental skills that separated them from their peers while still appealing to mainstream audiences. But in the beginning, an audience almost seemed like an afterthought. In their early years The Police and Green Day were hungry for success and would play nearly anywhere at any time, putting on inspired shows regardless of audience size. During The Police's first U.S. tour, their audiences were very small, but this did not prohibit them from performing as if there were thousands listening. Green Day's similar willingness to perform for any kind of crowd during their early years helped attract the attention of industry representative Rob Cavallo.

Cavallo worked as an A&R (artists and repertoire) representative for Warner Brothers Records, and he signed the band to Reprise Records (a subsidiary of Warner Brothers) in 1993. Green Day had released two previous albums, *39/Smooth* and *Kerplunk*, with a local record company. After their first album, drummer John Kiffmeyer unwisely chose to go to college, so their second album, *Kerplunk*, featured Tré Cool on drums. Now with funding and distribution provided by Warner Brothers, *Dookie* was released to great acclaim in 1994. Five singles—"She," "Longview," "Basket Case," "When I Come Around," and "Welcome to Paradise"—were on heavy rotation on mainstream radio stations as well as on MTV.

The success of *Dookie* can be partially attributed to the public's waning interest in grunge music. By 1994, grunge was mired in an endless loop of apathy, disenfranchisement, and corporate appropriation. Furthermore, with the suicide of Kurt Cobain, grunge had lost its most famous proponent. Admittedly, Green Day featured plenty of the same kinds of emotions and thoughts as their grunge antecedents, but they added an element of musical fun to being depressed and apathetic. Armstrong's distinctive vocal timbre combined with catchy melodies, meaningful lyrics, and Tré Cool's impressive drumming, created a sound that reinvigorated interest in punk music in the 1990s. Moreover, their playful videos and puckish personalities were perfect for MTV. Following Green Day's surprising success with *Dookie*, other pop/punk bands like Rancid and The Offspring were selling thousands of records and filling large venues. But this success had a downside; Green Day was accused of a cardinal sin within the world of punk . . . selling out.

The punk community ultimately criticized Green Day for merchandising outcast culture. After the success of *Dookie*, they were labeled as "traitors" and "sellouts." Green Day's most ardent supporters, and even some friends, had become more distant. In fact, Gilman Street had institutionalized anti-mainstream sentiment by barring performances from any band that managed to obtain a deal with a large record company. Of course, punk has been an element of the mainstream since the

1970s, so Green Day was simply creating music from that universal experience. Armstrong comments, "It's always been around, springing up in little suburban areas everywhere, wherever people grab ahold of it to express themselves. Now the media's grabbed ahold of it and is eating it up. Winona Ryder puts out *Reality Bites*, Beck puts out that song 'Loser.' Kurt Cobain blows his face off, River Phoenix croaks from an OD in front of a Hollywood nightclub. I think it's a sign of the times to be way more self-destructive, way more apathetic" (Lanham, 24). Of course, the punk community had also rejected The Police over a decade earlier. In their case, they were slightly older, not as politically driven, and possessed a higher level of musical skill than their punk counterparts. These were excellent grounds for exclusion, but The Police never truly wanted to be punks anyway. They used the rising popularity of punk as a vehicle for their own style and quickly jettisoned the punk aesthetic. Green Day *was* a part of this community, and their exclusion has been of interest to fans and journalists for years.

By the early 2000s, Green Day had lost some of its earlier momentum. Younger bands had taken Green Day's pop/punk formula and made it even more mainstream. Although their albums continued to sell well, they were no longer assured platinum record sales with every new release. But in 2004, Green Day debuted *American Idiot*. Bolstered by singles like "Holiday/Boulevard of Broken Dreams" "American Idiot," "Wake Me Up When September Ends," and "Jesus of Suburbia," the album became an international hit. Green Day had achieved a rare comeback in pop culture. Even more uncommon, *American Idiot* is a rock opera depicting the wanderings of Jesus of Suburbia, who travels to the big city and meets a series of characters. This extended format appears to be quite distanced from the punk-inspired tunes of *Dookie*, but in some regards, both albums connected to their listeners in similar fashions.

With some of the songs in *Dookie*, Green Day attracted both high and low culture. For instance, "Longview" features a roving bass line supporting a series of choruses and a bridge section that tacitly implores listeners to sing along. This pop sensibility harkens back to the finest work of The Beatles, a notable influence on Armstrong. Underneath these mainstream elements, though, the lyrics describe a desperate state of loneliness and isolation. The young protagonist, surely Armstrong himself, is trapped within a suburban world that offers no stimulus or challenges, and he is forced to self-medicate with marijuana and masturbation. Much like the finest examples of meaningful popular music, Green Day combines accessible mainstream pop sensibilities with serious content. Green Day used this method again while recording *American Idiot*. For instance, the tune "American Idiot" features a typical pop/punk arrangement of roaring guitars, fast tempos, and catchy melodies, but the lyrics are a scathing criticism of contemporary American politics. Indeed, much of the album is a mixture of pop-inspired backgrounds camouflaging rather meaningful and biting content. Of course, combining the low (pop/punk sensibilities) with high (political discussion) is an art that few highly successful mainstream artists have been able to manage.

The success of *Dookie* and *American Idiot* spawned a new generation of bands who use elements of Green Day's formula in their own music. Bands like Blink-182, Sum 41, Fall Out Boy, and Good Charlotte note Green Day as an early influence. Joel Madden, the lead singer of Good Charlotte, proclaimed, "[*Dookie*] changed my life. It made me want to start Good Charlotte. . . . Right after that record came out, we were like, 'We have to start a band in our garage right now and play shows . . . like Green Day" (D'Angelo). Contemporary bands like 5 Seconds of Summer, whose members were born around the time *Dookie* was released, have publicly expressed their debt to Green Day, and even Lady Gaga admits that the first album she ever bought was Green Day's *Dookie*.

Considering the musical challenges that accompany the rock trio, it is remarkable that anyone would bother to form one. Yet the vitality and visceral connections provided by the trio format, and popularized by The Police in the early 1980s, continues to attract those who are capable enough to operate on such a musical tightrope. Maybe this is the reason why these six trios are so highly regarded and influential. The requirements for operating within a trio are heightened to such an extent that, from the onset, the likelihood for musical success is increased. Nevertheless, these trios achieved the rare goal of being successful in the mainstream while maintaining a compelling historical position as well.

7

THE MUSIC AFTER THE POLICE

The Police were remarkable in many ways. Their rare combination of musical instincts, virtuosity, and marketing savvy led to immense popularity. Arguably, the most compelling aspect of The Police, though, is their prolific output after they broke up. There are few groups whose members, after reaching the pinnacle of stardom, continued to have rich and fulfilling musical careers. The post-Police work of Copeland, Summers, and Sting has been created with determination and creative honesty. Stewart Copeland has had a remarkably diverse career, ranging from film music to percussion ensembles. Andy Summers has immersed himself in the composition, virtuosity, and sonic imagery of the guitar. Of course, Sting has had the most visible post-Police career, yet even he has explored genres as diverse as Renaissance lute and English folk tunes. Each of these performers has repeatedly shown that there are no limits to their musical curiosity.

STEWART COPELAND

Stewart Copeland's post-Police oeuvre is impressively expansive and diverse, spanning film and television scores, ballet, opera, percussion ensembles, video game music, non-Western music, popular music, works for chamber orchestra, and numerous musical collaborations. Considering that Copeland was "only" a rock drummer, this is an impressive feat. Drummers are not historically regarded as the primary

creative force in most bands. In The Police, Sting, not Copeland, was
the primary songwriter and arranger, and thus the most likely candidate
for a post-Police career. In fact, it is uncommon for rock drummers to
have any sort of post-superstardom musical career, let alone a career
working within highly competitive and critically contested genres like
opera and ballet. And Copeland has not merely dabbled within these
genres; he has created a long-lived career scoring for film and television
projects as well as composing various kinds of Western art music. Moreover, Copeland has periodically returned to his rock roots with bands
like Animal Logic, Oysterhead, and Gizmo. Although his musical interests appear to be random, much of what he has created since The
Police has been based on earlier musical experiences. Copeland's musical journey is not the result of aimless wandering; rather, it is the product of musical foundations that were laid before The Police disbanded.

One of Copeland's early and little-known experiences with film music was in 1982 during the production of *Brimstone and Treacle*, star-
ring his bandmate, Sting. Sting invited Summers and Copeland to Abbey Road Studios to create some grooves for the film. Copeland admits
that he did not understand much about the process, and the film itself
may not have even been available during recording; nevertheless, portions of this session ("How Stupid Mr. Bates" and "A Kind of Loving")
became part of the album soundtrack. Later that year, Francis Ford
Coppola was looking for a percussionist/composer who could musically
illustrate elements of time in his newest film, *Rumble Fish*. Coppola's
son, Roman, suggested Copeland, who had a fortuitously planned tour
break in his schedule. Of course, Copeland had little experience with
film composition, but after a short audition in which he demonstrated
his ideas in front of scenes from the film, Coppola offered him the job.
Film scoring is a remarkably difficult skill that requires a breadth of
knowledge that spans orchestral arranging to complex computer soft-
ware. Copeland elaborates:

> When you work with film, you have to work with all kinds of different
> media. If you're a classical composer, you just work with orchestras.
> If you're in a rock band, you just work with rock bands. If you're a
> film guy, you've got to do everything. You've got to have rock music
> for this scene, you've got to have the orchestra swaying and heaving
> and making people cry in that scene. And then there's this other part
> of the movie where they go to Hong Kong and you have to come up

with Chinese music. The film composer is craft rather than art. You pick up skills there. The film composer has the widest set of musical skills of anyone. (Benz)

Most film composers refine their skills on low-budget films before they are prepared to work on a big-budget Coppola film, but Copeland's reputation as a superb rock drummer for one of the biggest bands in the world surely helped him get the job. In spite of his inexperience, Copeland charged into the "musical unknown" of film composing with a fearlessness typical of the Copeland family. Coppola's gamble paid off; the music for *Rumble Fish* was nominated for a Golden Globe Award for Best Original Score.

The success of the *Rumble Fish* soundtrack launched a remarkable career in film scoring. Copeland has since created music for such notable films as *Wall Street* and *9½ Weeks*, with his interest in film writing leading to television work as well. In 1985, Copeland and Derek Holt wrote the theme music for television's animated *Star Wars* spin-off titled *The Ewoks and the Droids* . At about the same time, Copeland began writing the music for multiple seasons of the CBS series *The Equalizer* (1986). Copeland would go on to create music for *Babylon 5* (1993), *Dead Like Me* (2003), and *Desperate Housewives* (2005), among many other shows. Even without considering the success Copeland attained while with The Police, his career as a film and television composer is remarkable.

Film scoring is loosely related to the Western art music tradition. Both genres make extensive use of orchestral elements, but that may be where the similarities end. Western art music has a very long and complex history that encompasses small and large musical genres, ranging from piano miniatures to twelve-hour operas. The music and artists of this musical world have been analyzed, judged, criticized, and venerated at great length for centuries. Unfortunately, this musical canon of elite and largely European composers generally marginalizes even the great film composers like John Williams, Danny Elfman, and Hans Zimmer. In other words, although a composer may use an orchestra, that does not qualify him or her to be admitted into the canon of Western art music. Nevertheless, the fearless Copeland has written a number of classical pieces, some of which were begun while he was officially still a member of The Police.

In 1986, Copeland was commissioned by the San Francisco Ballet to write a work based on Shakespeare's *King Lear*, which was followed by the ballet *Emilio* (1988), performed by the Trento Ballet in Italy, and *Prey* in 1994. Clearly not afraid of large-scale works, he also debuted his first opera, *Holy Blood and Crescent Moon*, in 1989. Apropos to Copeland's childhood in Lebanon, *Holy Blood* was a drama set during the Crusades. He continued his venture into opera with *Horse Opera* (1992), *The Cask of Amontillado* (1993), and *The Tell-Tale Heart* (2013). Considering Copeland's background, most audiences could justifiably assume that his operas are musically connected to rock music, but unlike rock operas such as The Who's *Tommy*, Copeland's works are more closely related to the traditions of Western art music. His operas, while not being overly long, employ the same orchestration and thematic techniques as those of canonic opera composers such as Giuseppe Verdi, Richard Wagner, and Giacomo Puccini. Copeland has also written symphonic works in the tradition set by some of his Western art music idols, Igor Stravinsky, Maurice Ravel, and Aaron Copland. Admittedly, Copeland's symphonic and chamber works, represented on albums like *Orchestralli* (2005), do not sound much like his musical inspirations, but these kinds of works should certainly be included in the discourse surrounding Western art music. He is justifiably proud of the work and dedication that has led to his growing orchestral oeuvre: "I played with rock bands for thirty years, and I love it, but you get ninety guys on the stage and that's pretty darn exciting. I like doing that. I learned the craft for that, the skill of getting those notes on the page, getting an orchestra to sound good" (Benz). Arguably, the most challenging aspect of working within the framework of Western art music is criticism, and there is little possibility that a well-known rock drummer such as Copeland could ever be reviewed objectively. Some critics, enamored with his rock status, are tempted to universally praise his music, while more conventional critics find fault in every facet of his compositional style. Of course, Copeland is aware of the critical storm that surrounds his works, so he has attempted to diffuse criticism by offering his own mock review:

> The world has gone completely mad. Cleveland Opera has sunk so low in its hunger for notoriety as to throw huge resources onto the lap of this entirely undeserving dilettante. Did I hear correctly that this man is the drummer (excuse me, "percussionist") of a pop

group? Surely in all the fine music schools there are young composers with the proper training who could have used these fine sets,
magnificent costumes, talented singers, brutalized orchestra, and
monumentally broad-minded conductor to give us an opera worthy
of the name. (*Strange Things Happen*, 95)

Even under the glare of never-ending criticism, Copeland has certainly
maintained his puckish sense of humor.

For an artist who is clearly proficient in so many genres of Western
music, it is remarkable that Copeland is comfortable within various
non-Western music styles as well. Although he was introduced to non-
Western music during his childhood, Copeland began his public journey into such music in 1985 with his film, *The Rhythmatist*. In the
summer of 1984, Copeland and director Jean-Pierre Dutilleux (who
worked with Sting years later) traveled through Kenya, Congo, Tanza-
nia, and Burundi filming a pseudo-improvisational movie detailing a
search for the roots of rock and roll. Copeland admits that *The Rhythmatist* was a unique endeavor:

> It made no sense whatsoever. I was trying to make a documentary,
> you know, like a meaningful, insightful examination of the African
> roots of American music. And the director, he was trying to make
> one kind of movie, which was an action-adventure thriller, and I was
> trying to make Richard Attenborough on acid. (Raz, "Stewart Cope-
> land")

Although the film and its soundtrack never achieved mainstream
success, it has become a cult favorite among Copeland fans and drummers. Copeland revisited exotic music in 2003 when he participated in
La Notte della Taranta. This festival, Italy's largest musical event, cele-
brates various combinations of Salento folk music. Every year a guest
artist, or "maestro concertatore," is invited to perform a series of concerts with a large group. The performances feature a blend of pop
melodies with intricate folk instruments and rhythms, and Copeland
viewed the performances on almost religious terms: "As I lope from the
stage to the palace dressing rooms my heart is full of joy. I'm not
religious but usually the thought in my head is one of gratitude. Thank
you Lord for this gift, this body, this life" (*Strange Things Happen*, 150).
In 2015, *Dare to Drum*, a documentary detailing Copeland's extensive

work with the eclectic percussion ensemble D'Drum premiered in Dallas, Texas. The film documents the remarkable dedication that he and his fellow musicians put into realizing Copeland's demanding composition "Gamelon D'Drum." Copeland worked for years on the project, which combined gamelon and various percussive instruments with a symphonic orchestra. The logistical and musical challenges were substantial, and few composers would be willing to take on such a time-consuming project, but the results were remarkably innovative and unique.

Of course, Copeland's earliest professional musical experiences were in popular music, and he has occasionally revisited this world. In 1987, he collaborated with famed jazz bassist Stanley Clarke and vocalist/songwriter Deborah Holland under the band name Rush Hour. In November of that year, they embarked on a short tour of South America with Copeland's former bandmate, Andy Summers. Summers, who was reluctant to join a group that would attract so many comparisons to The Police, quit the band after the tour ended in order to promote his own solo works. In 1989, Copeland and Clarke renamed their band Animal Logic and released their first studio album, also titled *Animal Logic*. Their follow-up album in 1991 was creatively titled *Animal Logic II*. Though Animal Logic was a promising concept, Copeland and Clarke were in high demand and unable to devote the considerable time and energy required to promote a new band. Nevertheless, Clarke and Copeland, who have known each other since the early 1970s, continue to work together. In fact, Copeland performed with Clarke as recently as 2014 on Clarke's album *Up*.

Following an extended hiatus from drumming, Copeland was asked by Les Claypool, the bassist for Primus, to join him and Trey Anastasio, the guitarist for Phish, for a one-time performance at the New Orleans Jazz & Heritage Festival in 2000. They named their new supergroup Oysterhead. Anastasio and Claypool's approach to performance was based on improvisation, something of which Copeland had little experience. Copeland's performance regimen had been defined by multiple rehearsals leading to a polished and practiced product, so playing with Oysterhead was a very different experience:

> I come from a world of pop music where improvisation in front of a
> paying audience is something that has to be surrounded by solid

material (songs). The idea of making it up as you go along is plain unprofessional. If you are just screwing around, how does the wardrobe lady backstage know which sequined jacket to bring out and when? How does the guitar tech know which guitar to have ready? Well, it turns out that Trey only uses one guitar for a show, and Les wears the same sequins all night. (*Strange Things Happen*, 120)

In 2001, Oysterhead released *The Grand Pecking Order*, but after a short tour the trio disbanded, largely because of time constraints.

The variety of genres to which Copeland has contributed, combined with his tireless work ethic, musical curiosity, and fearlessness, places him in a remarkably small number of pop musicians who have achieved personal and public success beyond life as a star with another band. Coincidently, Copeland's bandmates have followed similar creative paths.

ANDY SUMMERS

The Police were a storm of creativity, adoration, and turmoil, and after their dissolution, Andy Summers, for the first time in many years, was set adrift with few musical obligations. The marketing and economic capital accumulated by The Police enabled the bandmates to indulge in any musical curiosities they liked, and each of them exploited that capital in different ways. Nevertheless, independence does not always produce inspiration, and Summers clearly had to undergo an adjustment. When the band ultimately broke apart, he felt a sharp sense of irresolution: "For a long time I dreamed about the band as if somehow trying to rebuild it, or reclaim something stolen, or make it whole again. Somewhere on the subconscious level there was need for a closure" (*One Train Later*, 342). He dealt with the loss by pursuing his own musical interests: "Eventually I began to record a solo album, and the act of making music and being in the studio again felt like the first steps of healing and finding the direction forward" (*One Train Later*, 341). This solo album was titled *XYZ* (1987), and it stands out in Summers's oeuvre as his only post-Police attempt at mainstream success. *XYZ* was full of pop hooks, automated percussion, and Summers's David Byrne-inspired vocal timbre, but it did not attain mainstream commercial or critical acceptance. Although Summers later admitted that he had al-

ready outgrown the marketing and performance obligations of the popular music industry, it is understandable that he would attempt to re-
enter the pop mainstream. After all, he had just left one of the biggest
bands in the world, with all the accoutrements that come with it, and he
may have wanted try his hand at stardom on his own terms. Ultimately,
Summers was not going to find musical healing by being a pop vocalist,
so he refocused his career as a jazz instrumentalist.

Summers worked inside and outside of the traditional definitions of
jazz, combining non-Western musical styles, Brazilian styles, rock, mini-
malism, and improvisation with his unique concepts of sonic imagery.
Some of his albums are easy to label jazz while others are only vaguely
"jazzy," but in many regards, Summers's recordings defy definition. But
because most of his works are instrumental, they are typically classified
as jazz. Summers's relationship with the jazz community, though, is
complex. Critics and listeners of jazz place great emphasis on a canonic
repertoire and instrumental virtuosity, and while some of Summers's
works feature a great deal of these elements, some do not. This creates
an uneasy relationship between a creative and well-known artist and a
tradition-steeped musical community.

As a young man, Summers was an avid fan of American jazz musicians like Wes Montgomery, Thelonious Monk, Horace Silver, and
Miles Davis: "Although I still like Cliff Richard and the Shadows, *Kind
of Blue* and 'Goodbye Pork Pie Hat' make 'We're All Going on a Summer Holiday' seem like a piece of fluff" (*One Train Later*, 33). During
his formative years in Bournemouth, he played in local jazz bands, but
as he evolved into a professional guitarist in the 1960s, rock and blues
genres took precedence. Of course, there were always elements of jazz
in his work, from Dantalian's Chariot to The Police, but these elements
were inevitably subsumed by the requisite demands of rock. This is not
to say that Summers wasn't fully invested as the guitarist for The Police;
he definitely enjoyed the experience as a rock performer: "You start to
transcend everything. It becomes like one organism. The band and the
audience. . . . You channel this feeling. It's almost shamanic. It becomes
tribal" (*Better Than Therapy*). Nevertheless, in 1982 Summers returned to his instrumental roots and released the first of many instrumental albums, *I Advance Masked*.

The album was a collaborative effort between Summers and Robert
Fripp, best known for his work with King Crimson. It is awash in sonic

landscapes that are framed by minimalistic repetition and the occasional tuneful melody. There are no elaborate solo passages, swing feel, or nods to jazz repertoire or its improvisational language. By almost any definition, *I Advance Masked* is not jazz, but because it was an instrumental album, most critics judged it against the standard definitions of jazz. Chris Doering writes,

> Together they've created a rock version of ECM music out of lush guitar synthesizer textures, spare percussion, Fripp's polymath arpeggios and Summers's spacey chords. . . . Summers's romantic sensibilities make an excellent foil for Fripp's intellectual abstractions. . . . The Policeman's solos don't come off quite as well. (89)

Lynden Barber adds, "Summers, though proficient and undoubtedly effective with The Police, is in this context essentially dull" (18). Both reviewers see the album's lack of virtuosic passages as grounds for negative comments, but they have possibly missed the point of Summers's early instrumental offerings. Summers, in *I Advance Masked* and its follow-ups, *Bewitched* (1984) and *Mysterious Barricades* (1988), was not attempting to become another virtuosic guitar god; rather, he was approaching instrumental music with an emphasis on sonic imagery and composition, emphasizing timbre and arrangements over scalar improvisations. Summers has had an interest in visual imagery for decades, publishing four photography books (*Throb*, *I'll Be Watching You: Inside The Police*, *Light Strings*, and *Desirer Walks the Streets*) and participating in numerous photographic exhibitions, so his corresponding interest in sonic imagery certainly does not stem from an avoidance of virtuosity. In the end, Summers may have chosen this pseudo-jazz environment simply because it was the only musical world in which he was free to experiment with his ideas on sonic imagery and composition. Surely he knew that he would attract criticism from the jazz community.

By 1990, Summers began writing music reflecting contemporary jazz fusion. The albums *Charming Snakes* (1990), *World Gone Strange* (1991), and *Synaesthesia* (1995) feature aggressive melodies, beats, and improvisations, which sound similar to contemporary jazz groups like Spyro Gyra and Yellowjackets. These albums highlight some of the finest jazz musicians of the era such as Chad Wackerman, Victor Bailey, Herbie Hancock, Mark Isham, Bill Evans, and Mike Mainieri. Jazz critics cautiously applauded Summers's new sound:

> As if determined to enter the fusion-guitar hero sweepstakes along-
> side Allan Holdsworth and Frank Gambale, Summers wails on al-
> most every track. . . . There's a lot of guitar here. Personally, I didn't
> think Andy had it in him. I panned his textural New Agey fare. I
> applaud this noteworthy effort. The lad's got chops on top of being
> clever. (Milkowski, 32)

In other words, the more notes Summers played, the more jazz critics
approved of his work. Although Summers was now satisfying his jazz
audiences with angular melodies and driving beats, he continued to
pursue his interest in sonic imagery with tunes like "Passion of the
Shadow" and "Oudu Kanjaira."

With *The Last Dance of Mr. X* in 1997, Summers began to engage
with a more traditional jazz repertoire, performing versions of tunes by
revered jazz composers like Wayne Shorter and Horace Silver, and
even including a rare swing tune with "We See." Unfortunately, some in
the jazz community held on to their notions of "good" jazz:

> Andy Summers, despite a justifiable reputation as one of the most
> original and influential guitarists of the 1980s, is not the possessor of
> huge jazz chops . . . his single line work is rather ordinary . . .
> approaching several of these pieces as arrangements rather than
> blowing vehicles and striving to derive from them a song-like tonal-
> ity . . . once again it is curious not to hear more soloistic flair from
> such a renowned practitioner. (Gilbert, 38)

Indeed, Mark Gilbert is correct—Summers's compositions were not
"blowing vehicles" but represented carefully crafted compositional ex-
pressions. A year later, Summers recorded an entire album dedicated to
a single jazz composer, Thelonious Monk. Monk is one of the most
respected composers and performers in jazz history. His works are angular and lean, existing in the margins between consonance and disso-
nance. At least in the jazz world, performing Monk's work is treading on
sacred ground, so Summers included a personal anecdote within the
liner notes of *Green Chimneys*:

> I was sixteen when I first heard Monk's music. It knocked me out,
> got under my skin. It was jazz but it was something else, African—
> magical-cubist—primitive—Monk's world. At the time I was listen-
> ing hard to "Monk at the Town Hall." A friend loaned me his copy, I

loved it and spent many hours hunched over a Dansette trying to get my teenage fingers around those tunes. Monk came to England, I had to see him play. It was six hours on a cold train to London. I wasn't disappointed, he played solo piano, sandwiched between Dizzy Gillespie and Roy Eldridge. Monk took the music to another place altogether. His playing hit me in the gut—it was the essence, the distillation of jazz and the American life. A black and white movie. I couldn't talk about it then, only sense it—feel it. I have always loved Monk and his music, he created his own universe, one that has not only stood the test of time, but also been a wonderful inspiration. Thanks Monk!

As with many of Summers's prior releases, reaction was mixed from a jazz community fixated on scalar musical gymnastics: "The former Police guitarist is not the most nimble or studied of soloists, on jazz terms" (Woodard, 84). Ironically, Thelonious Monk himself had been criticized for his unconventional approach to composing and lack of virtuosic pedigree. In Monk's case, it took years for the jazz community to catch up with his musical innovations.

In 2000, Summers released *Peggy's Blue Skylight*, an album comprised of compositions by another jazz luminary, Charles Mingus. Once again, Summers was criticized for not only his use of sonic imagery but for playing the electric guitar: "Forget the harmonica and oboe; a case could be made that the electric guitar is the most obnoxious instrument in jazz. . . . The signature auras of several tracks are somewhat trite. Is that a chorus device painting his lines on the title cut? Whichever gizmo is being used, its electronic shimmer gets old quick" (Macnie, 60). Criticism aside, Summers continued to release albums on his own terms with a compelling series of guitar duo albums: *Invisible Threads with John Etheridge* (1994), *Strings of Desire with Victor Biglione* (1998), *Splendid Brazil with Victor Biglione* (2004), and *First You Build a Cloud with Ben Verdery* (2005). On the surface, the guitar duo format appears to be limiting, but Summers's duet albums are arguably his most compelling. Each album is a compendium of complex arrangements, sensitive accompaniments, deft improvisations, and lush sonic soundscapes. Recently, Summers released a remarkable album of Brazilian-inspired compositions with Fernanda Taki titled *Fundamental* (2012), which echoes the legendary albums of Antônio Carlos Jobim and Luiz Bonfá.

Admittedly, Andy Summers's post-Police career has included neither fame nor fortune. His tours include jazz festivals and clubs, not arenas, and his albums sell in the thousands, not millions. Moreover, working within the contested confines of jazz has proven to be challenging. But Summers has already experienced mainstream success, then relived it with the 2007 Police reunion, so he may no longer be seeking that kind of adoration. Instead, Summers can look back on a career dedicated to a set of musical ideals that he has doggedly pursued for decades.

STING

Sting has followed his musical journey in much the same way as his former bandmates. Immediately after the dissolution of The Police, he began an extraordinarily successful solo career based on a series of mainstream albums, beginning with *The Dream of the Blue Turtles* (1985) and spanning to *Sacred Love* (2003). These albums feature combinations of eclectic styles, sophisticated production, peerless musical arrangements, compelling lyrics, and unparalleled melodic sensibilities. Through these works, Sting attained the highest level of mainstream success while stretching the boundaries of pop music, but by 2003, he had "done it all." The popular music world no longer posed the same challenges and risks to Sting; even the 2007 Police reunion was based on repertoire he had created almost thirty years earlier. Risk has always been a vital component to his creativity: "How would I define creativity? For me, it's the ability to take a risk. To actually put yourself on the line and risk ridicule, being pilloried, criticized, whatever. But you have an idea that you think you want to put out there. And you must take that risk" (Raz, "How Do You Get Over"). In some regards, there were fewer risks for Sting to take in mainstream music, so he was no longer challenged creatively.

In 2006, Sting took on a new risk with *Songs from the Labyrinth*. This album primarily consists of Sting's versions of the works of John Dowland, a Renaissance lutenist and songwriter. This was certainly a bold move for the mainstream entertainer. Admittedly, other aging artists like Rod Stewart and Paul McCartney have experimented with jazz and classical genres, but Sting reached further back to an archaic time period. Even among Western-music scholars, there is comparatively little known about Dowland's work. Furthermore, Sting not only attempted to sing Dowland's songs, but to perform on the lute as well. The challenge of lute performance should not be underestimated, and few rock musicians have attempted it: "I think as guitarists we pick up a lute and it feels familiar, so we should be able to play it. . . . To play it you have to reconfigure the brain, which I think is good for musicians. We fall into patterns and habits. This opens up a whole different set of possibilities, musically and harmonically" (*The Journey & the Labyrinth*). Many critics categorized Sting's latest work as simply a vanity project, but this characterization may be unfair. Sting spent an extended period studying contemporary performances of Dowland, corresponding with Dowland scholars and, of course, spending countless hours practicing the lute. Sting clearly took this project seriously and considered it a labor of love. Keep in mind that Sting must have known that many would criticize his work, and indeed, comments like "Musically, there are horrid blotches that will cause the Dowland lover to wince" (Dye) were inevitable parts of the dialogue surrounding the recording. Nevertheless, Sting persisted and even proclaimed that he enjoyed the fact that his new musical curiosities were challenging for his listeners: "I like to surprise people. I don't want people to think, 'I know what the next Sting record is.' I really want people to be puzzled and challenged" (Dye). Indeed, the rest of Sting's career has been comprised of a series of challenges to his audiences.

Sting continued pursuing his musical interests with *If on a Winter's Night* . . . in 2009. Once again, he chose an unusual topic on which to base a recording. This time he composed and arranged a series of winter-themed tunes based on English ballads, fourteenth-century carols, lullabies, and traditional English songs. This contemplative music dealt with the mysticism and melancholy of the winter season. As is typical with Sting, the album was accompanied by a set of philosophies, one of which was based on the importance of melancholy: "In the winter we're asked to reflect on the ghosts of the past, on the year preceding. We must treat them calmly, civilly, and not run away from them. By doing that, we're allowed to move into the spring. It's very simple psychology. Our ancestors did that, and we still need to do it . . . animals hibernate, and we reflect" (Majoun). Indeed, melancholy pervades the album, but in a way, it lends a sense of maturity to it as well.

In 2010, Sting was invited by the Chicago Symphony to perform a benefit concert of his hits with the orchestra. He was intent on creating quality renditions of his tunes that would challenge the performers, as well as provide a satisfying experience for himself and the audience. The arrangements and resulting concert were successful enough that Sting decided to record an album of his orchestrated hits, titled *Symphonicities*. The resulting tour featured the Royal Philharmonic Orchestra playing compelling arrangements of Sting's greatest hits in orchestra halls around the world. At first glance, orchestral versions of rock hits could prove to be an eye-rolling experience, the last gasp of an aging rock star who has run out of new ideas, but *Symphonicities* deserves closer scrutiny. In fact, this album is a component of a decades-old dialogue involving the repertoire of The Police and Sting. Much like the jazz repertoire, the music of Sting and The Police has become the object of numerous versions in disparate styles.

In the world of jazz there is a canon, or repertoire, of revered songs, many of which have been performed for nearly a century. Standards like "All the Things You Are," "There Will Never Be Another You," and "Bye Bye Blackbird" have a melodic and harmonic structure that has proven to be conducive to jazz improvisation. For decades, versions of these songs, as with most of the jazz canon, have been re-recorded by countless musicians. Jazz artists take great care in tailoring their personal style to these tunes, and in fact, this personalization is a vital component of what makes jazz so compelling. In some regards, the music of Sting and The Police has developed a similar sort of repertoire.

Musicians from disparate backgrounds have actively engaged with the original recordings of The Police by re-recording them in sometimes radically different ways. In fact, the music of Sting and The Police has captured the musical imagination of so many individuals and groups that there are entire albums dedicated to new versions of their songs. In 1997 and 2000, ARK 21 records (founded by Miles and Stewart Copeland) released volumes one and two of *Reggatta Mondatta: A Reggae Tribute to The Police*. The albums feature prominent reggae artists such as Maxi Priest, Ziggy Marley, Pato Banton, and Steel Pulse remaking many iconic Police tunes. Decades ago, The Police were criticized for "stealing" reggae, but these tribute albums demonstrate that musical influences are a fluid movement from artist to artist and culture to culture. In this case, Jamaican reggae influenced The Police, and that influence produced a style and repertoire that has returned to Jamaica, forming a continuous cycle. But the influence of The Police reaches far beyond reggae. The album *Outlandos D'Americas: A Rock en Español Tribute to The Police* (1998) features a list of prominent Hispanic performers who incorporate various Latin American elements to the repertoire. Alternative bands have released multiple versions of Police tunes as well, with the albums *Many Miles Away* (2001) and *¡Policia!: A Tribute to The Police* (2005). There have been jazz albums honoring The Police (*The Jazz Tribute to Sting and The Police* [2002]), piano tributes (*Piano Tribute to Sting and The Police* [2014]), and even smooth jazz versions (*Sting: The Ultimate Tribute* [2004]). Each of these albums contributes to a dialogue of influence, and this dialogue is epitomized in the group's first hit, "Roxanne."

In 1997, the reggae group Aswad recorded a version of "Roxanne" for *Reggatta Mondatta*. Their version strips away the mystery of Roxanne and replaces it with a galloping and joyous feel, taking Roxanne from Paris and transporting her to Kingston. Later that year, the hip-hop impresario Puff Daddy recorded his own version of the song. Puff Daddy's version features a strong R&B flare with a vocal choir, piano fills, and a string section combined with a series of rap verses bookending Sting's chorus, which has been significantly slowed down. If "Roxanne" were recorded in Brooklyn in the late 1990s, this is what it would have sounded like. Two years later, another pop icon, George Michael, recorded "Roxanne" for his *Songs from the Last Century* album. Michael returns Roxanne to her promiscuous roots by creating a sensuous jazz version of the tune. But in Michael's version, the protagonist no longer demands that Roxanne "put away her makeup"; instead, he charms her into giving up her wanton ways. A surprising contributor to the "Roxanne" dialogue is rapper Cam'ron. In 2000, Cam'ron sampled the most iconic element of "Roxanne," the distinctive guitar introduction, and incorporated it into "What Means the World to You." Cam'ron's syncopated rap verses cleverly dance above Summers's repeated guitar pattern. Cam'ron, though, takes a unique view of "Roxanne." Rather than begging a woman to change her ways, Cam'ron, in fact, proclaims that he's looking for even more "Roxannes." Throughout the track, Cam'ron boasts of his sexual powers and pleads for women to "just come lift up that dress for now." In 2001, the innovative film *Moulin Rouge!* featured a hybrid version of "Roxanne" titled "El Tango de Roxanne," which included a combination of the original melody with authentic tango rhythms. Brilliantly playing on the original version's tango origins, "El Tango" is aggressively sexual and exotic, and highlights some of the best characteristics of the original. The American rock band Fall Out Boy recorded their version of "Roxanne" in 2003. Fall Out Boy's version harkens to the punk origins of The Police. Their version is loud, dissonant, and full of youthful energy, much like The Police were in the late 1970s. Finally, Sting's own version of "Roxanne" in *Symphonicities* is a sophisticated product resulting from decades of performances. The rough edges of the original have been smoothed over by Sting's peerless vocals. The orchestra, with its contrapuntal strings and soaring winds, provides a sophistication and maturity that suits Sting at this point in his career.

The case of "Roxanne" demonstrates that music lives on in an endless dialogue of versions and, ultimately, influences. It is a dialogue between artists, musical communities, and even geographic regions, but most importantly, it is a dialogue between generations. Just as with jazz, older generations pass down their renditions of a "sacred repertory" to younger generations, with each generation contributing to the dialogue in equal and unique ways. The same phenomenon has happened, and continues to occur, with the music of The Police. Summers, Copeland, and Sting remain viable performers and are themselves participants in the dialogue that they initiated.

In 2009 Sting commented, "Music is a journey that never quite ends. There's always something new to learn. There's always something more and more. You know, it's composition or harmony. It's an endless journey" (Simon). Indeed, Andy Summers, Sting, and Stewart Copeland began a communal musical journey in 1977, which has yet to conclude. All three artists have shown that they view music as a journey, but each of them has taken different steps in that journey. Moreover, each bandmate has remained an actively creative entity. While there are those who may criticize their artistic choices, each musician has shown a regard for satisfying his individual musical curiosity above all else. In the end, we all take journeys in life, sometimes communal, sometimes solitary, but artists like The Police remind us that we are never really alone.

FURTHER READING

"Against All Odds." *Live Aid*. Prod. Kate Werran. BBC. 13 July 2010. Television.
All This Time. A&M Records, December 2001. DVD. A heartfelt performance in Tuscany on September 11, 2001. Sting opens the show with "Fragile" and dedicates it to those who died in the terrorist attacks.
Band Aid: The Song That Rocked the World. Dir. Melissa FitzGerald. BBC Three. October 2004. Television. This is a well-researched documentary on Band Aid.
Barber, Lynden. "Review of *I Advance Masked*." *Melody Maker*. 2 October 1982: 18. Print.
Beck, Marilyn. "Poor Sell of Rockumentary Stings Director." *Chicago Tribune*. 5 December 1985. Print.
Bendjelloul, Malik. "Interview with Sting." SVT. 2010. Television.
Benz, Steve. *The Blend*. WSDI, Chicago. 20 December 2013. Radio.
Berklee College of Music Commencement. "Sting's Commencement Speech." 15 May 1994. Web. Sting was honored to address such a prestigious music school. He offers advice and speaks about his childhood.
Berryman, James. *Sting and I*. London: John Blake Publishers, 2005. Print. This book was written by one of Sting's oldest friends. It contains humorous anecdotes and sheds light on Sting's private life.
Better than Therapy: Living The Police Reunion. Dir. Jordan Copeland. A&M Records/Polydor Limited, 2008. DVD. A short, but entertaining, behind-the-scenes view of The Police reunion tour.
Beware of Mr. Baker. Dir. Jay Bulger. Insurgent Media, 2012. DVD. This video narrates the life and times of one of rock's most colorful characters, Ginger Baker.
Breskin, David. "Bob Geldof: The Rolling Stone Interview." *Rolling Stone*. 5 December 1985: 26+. Print.
Bring on the Night. Dir. Michael Apted. A & M Video, 2005. DVD. This video was created to promote Sting as a solo artist. It concludes with the birth of his son, Jake, and a triumphant performance.
Brooks, Cody. "Where's Sting?" *AND* Magazine. 8 April 2012. Web.
Campion, Chris. *Walking on the Moon: The Untold Story of the Police and the Rise of New Wave Rock*. Hoboken, NJ: John Wiley & Sons, 2010. Print. Campion's book tells the tale of The Police and the world in which they created their music. It is well written, and the anecdotes are very entertaining.
Cateforis, Theo. *Are We Not New Wave?: Modern Pop at the Turn of the 1980s*. Ann Arbor: University of Michigan Press, 2011. Print. Cateforis's book is the definitive work on new wave music.

Chao, Georgia T., and Henry Moon. "The Cultural Mosaic: A Metatheory for Understanding the Complexity of Culture." *Journal of Applied Psychology* 90.6 (2005): 1128–40. Print.

Cinequest Film Festival. "Interview with Stewart Copeland." 3 March 2007. Web. This extensive interview was part of Copeland's promotion of his documentary, *Everyone Stares*. Copeland's discussions are thoughtful and articulate.

Clapton, Eric. "Cream: Rock and Roll Hall of Fame Induction." 12 January 1993. Television.

Clarkson, Wensley. *A Tale in the Sting*. London: John Blake Publishers, 2003. Print.

"Classic Albums: Disraeli Gears." Dir. Matthew Longfellow. VH1. 2006. Television.

Connelly, Christopher. "Record Review of The Secret Policeman's Ball." *Rolling Stone*. 13 May 1982: 67–68. Print.

Copeland, Ian. *Wild Thing*. New York: Simon and Schuster, 1995. Print. Ian Copeland's autobiography is full of colorful anecdotes and reveals that, like most of his family, he was a trailblazer.

Copeland, Stewart. *Strange Things Happen*. New York: HarperCollins, 2009. Print. This autobiography is more a collection of amusing stories than a full-fledged narrative of Copeland's life. It is very entertaining and mandatory reading for Copeland fans.

D'Angelo, Joe. "How Green Day's *Dookie* Fertilized A Punk-Rock Revival." Mtv.com/news. 15 September 2004. Web.

DeCurtis, Anthony. "Sting Debuts New Band." *Rolling Stone*. 14 January 1988: 23. Print.

Do They Know It's Christmas?—The Story of the Official Band Aid Video. Phonogram Limited, 1984. Videocassette.

Doering, Chris. "Review of *I Advance Masked*." *Musician*. November 1982: 88–89. Print.

Donaton, Scott. *Madison and Vine: Why the Entertainment and Advertising Industries Must Converge to Survive*. New York: McGraw-Hill, 2004. Print.

Dutilleux, Jean-Pierre, and Sting. *Jungle Stories: The Fight for the Amazon*. London: Barrie and Jenkins, 1989. Print. This picture book was published as a fund-raiser for Sting's Rainforest Foundation. It contains excellent photos and narratives written by Sting and others.

Dye, David. "Sting: From The Police to the Elizabethan Era." *World Cafe*. NPR. 24 November 2006. Radio.

Everyone Stares: The Police Inside Out. Dir. Stewart Copeland. Universal, 2006. DVD. Copeland's film features the early days of The Police. It should be mandatory viewing for any Police fan.

Fitzpatrick, Rob. "Rush: Our Fans Feel Vindicated." *Guardian*. 24 March 2011. Web.

Fricke, David. "Bob Geldof: Rock & Roll's World Diplomat." *Rolling Stone*. 18 July 1985: 18+. Print.

Fricke, David. "Caravan For Human Rights." *Rolling Stone*. 19 June 1986: 59+. Print.

Gambaccini, Paul. "Interview with The Police" ca. 1983. Web.

Geldof, Bob, and Paul Vallely. *Is That It?* Middlesex: Penguin, 1986. Print. This is Geldof's autobiography, telling the story of his remarkable life.

Gilbert, Mark. "Review of *Last Dance of Mr. X*." *Jazz Journal International*. October 1998: 38. Print.

Greene, Andy. "How Amnesty International Rocked the World: The Inside Story." Weblog post. *Rolling Stone*. 25 October 2013. Web.

Gross, Terry. "Billie Joe Armstrong, from Green Day to Broadway." *Fresh Air*. NPR. 27 May 2010. Radio.

Gumbel, Bryant. "Today Show Interview with Sting, Peter Gabriel, Bill Graham, and Jack Healey." *Today*. NBC. 16 June 1986. Television.

Harris, Steve, and Osamu Masui. "Sting Interview Part 1." 9 August 1985. Web.

Hebdige, Dick. *Cut 'N' Mix: Culture, Identity and Caribbean Music*. New York: Methuen & Co., 1987. Print. Hebdige's research on Caribbean music is highly regarded in academic circles.

Holland, Jools. "Police in Montserrat (1981)" in *Every Breath You Take: The DVD*. A&M Records, 2002. DVD. Holland's rapport with his old friends led to an informal and sometimes revealing series of interviews during the recording for *Ghost in the Machine*. Holland also includes footage of Montserrat and its inhabitants.

Interview of The Police by French Journalist. ca. 1983. Web.

Interview of The Police on Swedish Television. 1 January 1979. Television.

The Journey & The Labyrinth. Dir. Ann Kim and Jim Gable. UMG Recordings, 2007. DVD. This video accompanies Sting's *Songs from the Labyrinth*. It provides excellent backstories to the complex songs.

Laing, Dave. *One Chord Wonders: Power and Meaning in Punk Rock*. Philadelphia: Open University Press, 1985. Print.

Lanham, Tom. "Generation Why: Green Day Wakes Up and Smells the Coffee." *Musician*. September 1994: 22–24. Print.

Letts, Don. "Black-White: Interview with Don Letts." In *Sniffin' Glue: The Essential Punk Accessory*. London: Sanctuary, 2000. Print. This interview is included in this compilation of the punk fanzine, "Sniffin' Glue."

Letts, Don. "Don Letts Interviewed in London 2010." Red Bull Music Academy. 3 February 2014. Web.

Lynskey, Dorian. "U2, Bruce Springsteen, Live Aid, and the Difficult Art of Stadium Protest." In 33 *Revolutions Per Minute: A History of Protest Songs, From Billie Holiday to Green Day*. New York: HarperCollins, 2011. Print.

Macnie, Jim. "Review of *Peggy's Blue Skylight*." *Downbeat*. November 2000: 60–61. Print.

Majoun, Michaela. "Sting: Making Music for a Winter's Night." *World Cafe*. NPR. 24 December 2009. Radio. Many of Sting's NPR interviews go into more depth than the typical radio interview.

"The Making of Band Aid, 'Do They Know It's Christmas?'" *Part Nine – The Master Tapes— with Midge Ure*. BBC Radio One. 24 November 1994. Radio.

Maloof, Rich. *Jim Marshall: The Father of Loud*. Milwaukee: Hal Leonard, 2004. Print.

McBride, Christian. "Sting Interview." Conversations with Christian. 2009. Web. McBride has recorded and toured with Sting many times, and Sting was comfortably candid.

McMullen, Jeff. "Interview with Sting." *60 Minutes, Australia*. CBS. 1996. Television.

Milkowski, Bill. "Review of *Charming Snakes*." *Downbeat*. January 1991: 32. Print.

Morris, Chris. "Small Means Big for Miles Copeland." *Rolling Stone*. 3 April 1980: 24–25. Print.

Moskowitz, David. *Caribbean Popular Music: An Encyclopedia of Reggae, Mento, Ska, Rock Steady, and Dancehall*. Westport, Conn: Greenwood Press, 2005. Print.

O'Brien Chang, Kevin, and Wayne Chen. *Reggae Routes: The Story of Jamaican Music*. Philadelphia: Temple University Press, 1998. Print.

Outlandos to Synchonicities. PolyGram Video, 1995. DVD.

Paxman, Jeremy. "Sting Interview." *Newsnight*. 1 December 2009. Television.

Pozner, Vladimir. "Sting Interview." *Pozner Show*. Channel One. December 2010. Television. Pozner is an excellent interviewer and asks Sting questions that few other interviewers have.

Ragogna, Mike. "And Now for Something Completely Different: The Secret Policeman's Film Festival." *Huffington Post*. 12 June 2009. Web.

Raz, Guy. "How Do You Get Over Writer's Block?" *NPR TED Radio Hour*. NPR. 3 October 2014. Radio. Sting discusses his career-long battle with writer's block.

Raz, Guy. "Stewart Copeland: A Life of Misadventure." *All Things Considered*. NPR. 4 October 2009. Radio.

Roby, Steven, and Brad Schreiber. *Becoming Jimi Hendrix: From Southern Crossroads to Psychedelic London*. New York: Da Capo, 2010. Print.

Rock Milestones: Reggatta de Blanc. Classic Rock Legends, 2007. DVD.

"Rockin' All Over the World." *Live Aid*. Dir. Janice Sutherland. 13 July 2010. Television. This well-researched documentary narrates the chaos leading up to Live Aid.

"Rolling Stone Music Awards." *Rolling Stone*. 1 March 1984: 18–19. Print.

Rush: Beyond the Lighted Stage. Dir. Sam Dunn and Scot McFadyen. Banger Films, 2010. DVD. This is one of the finest documentaries on Rush. If you are a Rush fan, you must watch it.

Sandford, Christopher. *Sting: Demolition Man*. New York: Carroll and Graf, 1998. Print.

Savage, Jon. *England's Dreaming: Anarchy, Sex Pistols, Punk Rock, and Beyond.* New York: St. Martin's Griffin, 2001. Print. Savage is one of the most compelling writers of the punk movement.

Simon, Scott. "Music for Sting's Favorite Season." *Weekend Edition Saturday.* NPR. 7 November 2009. Radio.

Stefani, Gwen. "Rock and Roll Hall of Fame Induction Ceremony." 10 March 2003. Television.

Stewart, John. "Nevermind Twentieth Anniversary." Sirius/XM. 24 September 2011. Radio.

Sting. *Broken Music: A Memoir.* New York: Dial, 2003. Print. Sting's autobiography is remarkably well written and reveals his early life and inspirations.

Sting. Liner notes, . . . *Nothing Like the Sun.* A&M Records, 1987. CD.

Sting. *Lyrics by Sting.* New York: Dial , 2007. Print. Sting provides the inspirations and the correct lyrics for nearly all of his songs.

Sting: Behind the Music. Prod. Paul Barrosse. VH1. 26 September 1999. Television.

Sting: MTV Rockumentary. Prod. Jonathan Bendis. MTV. 29 June 1991. Television.

Sting Unplugged. A&M Video, 1992. DVD.

Sting: VH1 Storytellers. Dir. Michael Simon. VH1. 1996. Television. Sting discusses the backstories of many of his biggest hits. The performances are excellent as well.

Summers, Andy. "Interview with Andy Summers at the Experience Music Project." 18 October 2006. Web. Summers is comfortable and candid in this extensive interview that covers everything from The Police to his love of photography.

Summers, Andy. *One Train Later.* New York: Thomas Dunne Books, 2006. Print. Much like the autobiographies of his bandmates, this is mandatory reading for Police fans. Summers's stories are absolutely mesmerizing.

Swenson, John. Liner notes, *Rush: Chronicles.* Mercury Records, 1990. CD.

Tamarkin, Jeff. *Aquarian.* 1 January 1979. Print.

Tannenbaum, Rob. "Bob Geldof." *Rolling Stone.* 15 November 1990: 74+. Print.

Tannenbaum, Rob. "Miles Copeland." *Musician.* March 1988: 28–32. Print.

"Top U.S., U.K. Talent in Tour." *Billboard.* 16 August 1975: 70. Print.

Ure, Midge. "Interview with Midge Ure and Bob Geldof." ca. 1985. Web.

Ure, Midge. *Midge Ure, If I Was . . .: The Autobiography.* London: Virgin, 2004. Print.

VH1 Classic Albums: Nevermind. Dir. Bob Smeaton. 2004. Television.

VH1 News Special: Grunge. VH1. 13 September 2001. Television.

"Video Killed the Radio Star: Duran Duran." Prod. Scott Millaney. *Video Killed the Radio Star: The Artist's View.* AXS TV. 14 June 2014. Television.

"Video Killed the Radio Star: Sting." Prod. Scott Millaney. *Video Killed the Radio Star: The Artist's View.* AXS TV. 14 June 2014. Television. This program provides commentary from Sting and Kevin Godley on the making of music videos.

Woodard, Josef. "Review of *Green Chimneys.*" *Jazztimes.* November 1999: 84. Print.

FURTHER LISTENING

Note: This is not a complete discography of The Police. Their five studio albums are included, but the many "best of" albums have been excluded. Furthermore, Andy Summers, Stewart Copeland, and Sting are especially prolific individual artists, and only select albums have been included. Lastly, there are numerous live performance videos, and although many of these videos are very entertaining, only a select few have been included.

Outlandos d'Amour (November 1978), album, A&M Records
This first album is a product of the punk environment in which it was created. Tunes like "Next to You" and "Truth Hits Everybody" are pure punk anthems. Likewise, "Roxanne" and "Can't Stand Losing You" will become a permanent part of The Police's concert repertoire. The album is bursting with youthful energy and potential.

Reggatta de Blanc (October 1979), album, A&M Records
This album introduced the world to the band's deft style hybrids, virtuosic performing, and catchy hooks. "Message in a Bottle" and "Walking on the Moon" are exemplars of this sophisticated style mixing and pop melodic sensibility. Much like their first album, *Reggatta* was recorded on a limited budget, and that is reflected in the equally lean compositions.

Zenyatta Mondatta (October 1980), album, A&M Records

The Police recorded *Zenyatta* in less than a month because of their unrelenting tour schedule. The day after the album was completed, The Police were back on the road. This may be their most critically maligned album, but it still produced the hits "Don't Stand So Close to Me" and "De Do Do Do, De Da Da Da."

Ghost in the Machine (October 1981), album, A&M Records
The band was already experiencing artistic differences, and even the album cover was a compromise featuring a digital representation of Copeland, Summers, and Sting. Sting's songwriting skills were maturing, and he was looking for the artistic input of his bandmates less often. Nevertheless, *Ghost* featured the three hits, "Every Little Thing She Does Is Magic," "Invisible Sun," and "Spirits in the Material World."

I Advance Masked (October 1982), album, A&M Records
The album is a collaborative effort between Summers and Robert Fripp, best known for his work with King Crimson. The album is awash in sonic landscapes that are framed by minimalistic repetition and the occasional tuneful melody.

The Police: Around the World (February 1983), video, A&M Records
This video documents the first world tour of The Police. It presents the band as a fun-loving group of musicians travelling through exotic locations. It was part of a remarkable marketing campaign to position The Police as a worldwide phenomenon.

Synchronicity (June 1983), album, A&M Records
This album was the band's biggest seller and one of the most iconic albums of the 1980s. The singles "Every Breath You Take," "King of Pain," and "Wrapped around Your Finger" became anthems of FM rock radio and were placed on heavy rotation on MTV. *Synchronicity* proved to many that The Police was the biggest band in the world.

Rumble Fish: Original Motion Picture Soundtrack (November 1983), album, A&M Records
This was Stewart Copeland's first attempt at film scoring. It was a success; he was nominated for a Golden Globe Award for the score.

The Dream of the Blue Turtles **(June 1985), album, A&M Records**
Sting's debut solo album featured elite jazz artists performing compelling pop material. This album thrust Sting into the limelight as a solo performer with hits like "If You Love Somebody Set Them Free," "Fortress around Your Heart," and "Love is the Seventh Wave."

Every Breath You Take: The Singles **(November 1985), album, A&M Records**
The bandmates were no longer able to operate as a viable creative force, so they decided to re-record some of their hits. Even this proved to be too much. The only new song in this compilation album is a remake of "Don't Stand So Close to Me '86."

Bring on the Night **(October 1985), video, A&M Records**
This film details the rehearsals and preparations for Sting's first solo concert and tour. It includes multiple interviews with Sting's new band, as well as with Miles Copeland. It was an obvious attempt to capture a more mature and sophisticated audience. At its conclusion, Sting's son, Jake, is born.

Bring on the Night **(July 1986), album, A&M Records**
This remarkable double album features one of Sting's best bands. The arrangements provide lots of room for the musicians to show off their unique skills, yet the tunes are never lost in the "jazz translation."

. . . Nothing Like the Sun **(October 1987), album, A&M Records**
This could be Sting's finest solo album. The stylistic and narrative range is impressive, ranging from the pop-styled "We'll Be Together" to the puckish "Englishman in New York" to the meaningful "Fragile." Sting reaches a level of musical and lyrical sensibility with *Nothing* that he could not have attained with The Police.

Animal Logic **(October 1989), album, I.R.S. Records**
The band was comprised of singer Deborah Holland, jazz bassist Stanley Clarke, and Stewart Copeland. Holland was the primary songwriter, but her bandmates provided a steady and compelling instrumental setting. They released a follow-up album, titled *Animal Logic II*, in 1991.

Charming Snakes (1990), album, Private Music
Andy Summers's album is a fine example of nineties jazz fusion. The performers are first rate, and the compositions are angular, complex, and remarkably aggressive. Summers will release albums similar to *Charming* throughout the decade.

Soul Cages (January 1991), album, A&M Records
Sting's third solo album was dedicated to his father, who had died in 1989. Sting's relationship with his father was complex, and Sting attempted to work out some of those issues through song. Although the album included some pop-styled singles like "All This Time," most of the content is melancholic and introspective. Sting will return to some of these themes in *The Last Ship*.

Ten Summoner's Tales (March 1993), album, A&M Records
This album was Sting's return to upbeat and fun pop songs. Nearly every tune has a catchy hook. There is even a nod to American country music with "Love Is Stronger than Justice (The Munificent Seven)." One of Sting's most iconic tunes, "Fields of Gold," is also included.

Message in a Box: The Complete Recordings (September 1993), box set, A&M Records
Although there are a few foreign language versions missing, this box set contains the complete studio recordings of The Police. This may be the best choice for the casual Police fan.

Klark Kent: Kollected Works (1995), album, Capitol Records
In the late 1970s, Copeland had recorded a number of tunes under the alias Klark Kent. In 1980, Copeland released an album of these tunes titled *Klark Kent: Music Madness from The Kinetic Kid*. The tunes are excellent examples of early new wave music. Tunes like "Strange Things Happen" and "Don't Care" are short and surprisingly catchy. *Kollected Works* is a compilation of those tunes.

Synaesthesia (1995), album, CMP Records
Summers enlists the legendary drummer Ginger Baker to provide a spirited background to Summers's sonic images. This album features a

mix of non-Western music, Afro-Cuban grooves, and even a string quartet.

The Police Live! (June 1995), album, A&M Records
This double album features early and late performances of The Police. The first is from a Boston show in 1979. The band is raw and still evolving from their punk influences. The second performance is from a two-night engagement in Atlanta in 1983. The Police are more polished, and they are clearly enjoying being the biggest band in the world.

Mercury Falling (March 1996), album, A&M Records
Although not as upbeat as *Ten Summoner's Tales*, it features another country song, "I'm So Happy I Can't Stop Crying," which would be a hit for Toby Keith in late 1997.

Strontium 90: Police Academy (August 1997), album, ARK 21
This album features a performance from May 28, 1977, by bassist Mike Howlett, Copeland, Sting, and Summers, known collectively as Strontium 90. This was the first time that Summers performed with Sting and Copeland. After this concert, they changed their name to the Elevators, but after a couple more performances, they disbanded.

Green Chimneys: The Music of Thelonious Monk (May 1999), album, RCA Victor
This is Summers's tribute to the music of the legendary jazz pianist, Thelonious Monk. Although Monk's music is sacred ground in the jazz world, Summers's arrangements convey a sense of respect and love. He even convinced Sting to join him on "Round Midnight."

Brand New Day (September 1999), album, A&M Records
Brand New Day was heralded as Sting's comeback album. Millions of copies were sold around the world, largely fueled by the single "Desert Rose." The tune, featuring Algerian singer Cheb Mami, was used in a cross-promotional Jaguar commercial and became a worldwide hit.

Peggy's Blue Skylight (September 2000), album, RCA Victor

Much like *Green Chimneys*, Summers's *Peggy's Blue Skylight* is a tribute to another jazz luminary, Charles Mingus. Summers is clearly pay-
ing his debt to the traditional jazz repertoire.

The Grand Pecking Order (October 2001), album, Elektra Records

Following a hiatus from drumming, Copeland was asked by Les Claypool, the bassist for Primus, to join him and Trey Anastasio, the guitarist
for Phish, for a one-time performance at the New Orleans Jazz & Heritage Festival in 2000. They named their new supergroup Oysterhead.
The Grand Pecking Order was their first and only album. There have
been persistent rumors that the group will re-form at some point.

Sacred Love (September 2003), album, A&M Records

Once again, Sting experiments with various genres. This album features
R&B, soul, electronic dance music, and rock. His duet with Mary J.
Blige on "Whenever I Say Your Name" is particularly compelling.

Songs from the Labyrinth (October 2006), album, Deutsche Grammophon

This album primarily consists of Sting's interpretations of the works of
John Dowland, a Renaissance lutenist and songwriter. Sting spent an
extended period studying performances of Dowland, corresponding
with Dowland scholars, and countless hours practicing the lute.

The Stewart Copeland Anthology (August 2007), album, Koch Records

This is an excellent compilation for the casual fan of Stewart Copeland.
It spans works from Klark Kent to the theme music for the video game
Spyro the Dragon.

If on a Winter's Night . . . (October 2009), album, Deutsche Grammophon

This album is a collection of newly composed and arranged winter-
themed tunes based on English ballads, fourteenth-century carols, lullabies, and traditional English songs. This contemplative music deals
with the mysticism and melancholy of the winter season.

Symphonicities (August 2010), album, Deutsche Grammophon
This album is comprised of orchestral arrangements of Sting's and The Police's greatest hits. The arrangements provide a new take on some old hits, and Sting's voice is peerless.

Fundamental (September 2012), album, Polysom Records
This is a remarkable album of Brazilian-inspired compositions with vocalist Fernanda Taki, which echoes the legendary albums of Antonio Carlos Jobim and Luiz Bonfá. Summers's music is elegant and sophisticated.

The Last Ship (September 2013), album, Cherrytree/Interscope/A&M Records
This album contains some of the music featured in Sting's Broadway show, *The Last Ship*. The album was the first since *Sacred Love* to be entirely composed by Sting. The songs are inspired by Sting's childhood and his upbringing in Wallsend.

INDEX

ABOUT THE AUTHOR

Aaron J. West has been a professional musician since he was fifteen years old. He has performed with jazz and pop legends such as Arturo Sandoval, Brian Wilson, Norah Jones, and the Glenn Miller Orchestra. He released his first solo album in 2007, titled *Colors and Angles.* He has written numerous articles on jazz and popular music and is currently a professor of music history at Collin College. He is a racquetball and mud run enthusiast who lives with his wife, a music librarian and flautist, in Frisco, Texas.

31901056721790